Six-Figure Freelance Writer

Six-Figure Freelance Writer

A HOLISTIC GUIDE ON FINDING
FREEDOM IN FREELANCING

BY AMY SUTO

All client and project details in this book have been fictionalized, and any resemblance to real-life individuals or projects is coincidental. In addition, the information provided in this book is for educational purposes only. It is not intended to be a source of financial or legal advice. The publisher and the author make no guarantee of financial results obtained by using this book.

Copyright © 2023 Sutoscience LLC

All rights reserved. No part of this book may be reproduced or used in any manner without written permission of the copyright owner except for the use of quotations in a book review. For more information, address: amy@amysuto.com

First Edition: March 2023

Book cover and interior design by Ashley Munson of Libra Collective
Edited by Kyle Cords
Proofreading by Dana Alsamsam

ISBN 9798377077831

Published by Sutoscience LLC
amysuto.com

for Kyle

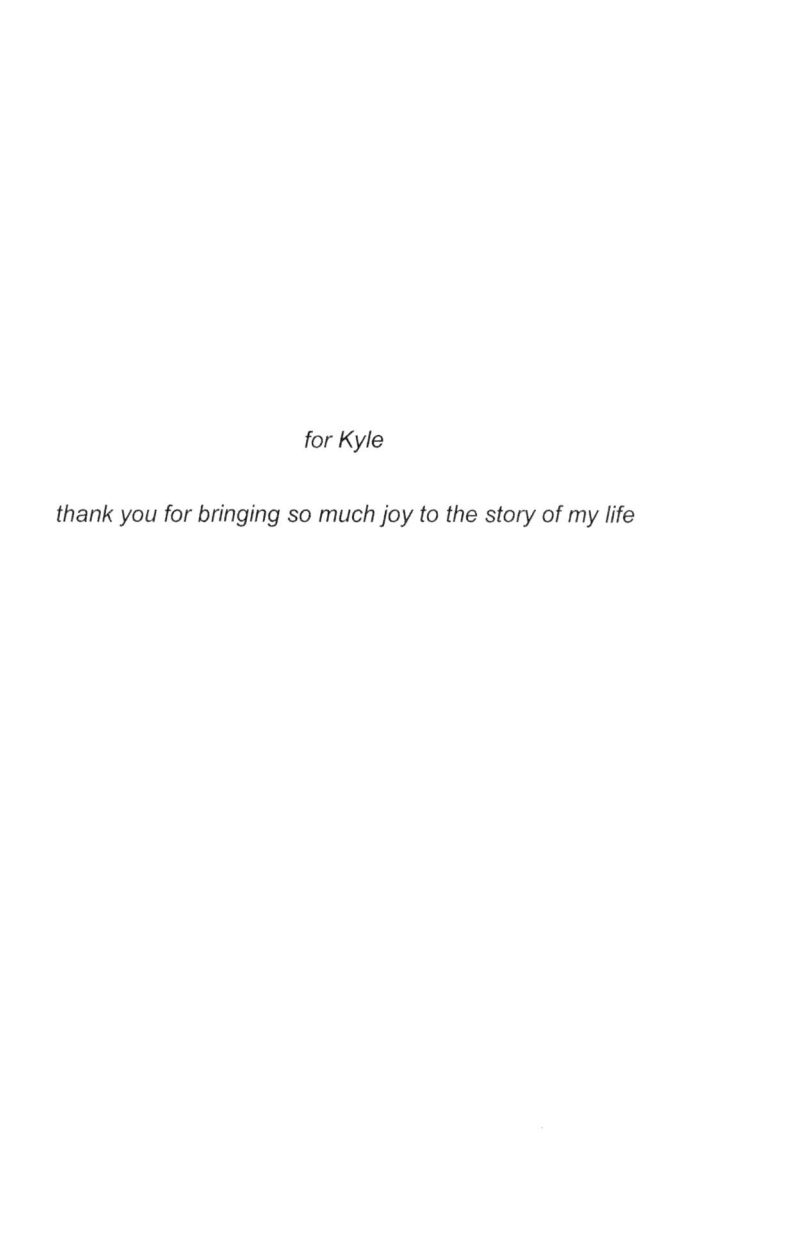

thank you for bringing so much joy to the story of my life

TABLE OF CONTENTS

✴ **Introduction** — 1

✴ **Part 1: Getting Started as a Freelance Writer** — 7

Chapter 1: Checklist for New Freelance Writers — 11

Chapter 2: Picking a Freelance Writing Niche — 13

Chapter 3: Building Your Bio and Taking Your Headshot — 23

Chapter 4: Calculating Your Hourly Rate — 31

Chapter 5: How to Price Your Projects and Get Paid More — 39

Chapter 6: How to Build Your Freelance Writing Portfolio — 47

Chapter 7: Freelance Platforms and Finding Great Clients — 53

Chapter 8: Taking the Call: Landing a Client — 61

Chapter 9: No Blog No Life: Building Your Freelancing Website — 71

Chapter 10: Project Tracking and Energy Management — 77

Chapter 11: Handling Difficult Situations with Clients — 91

Chapter 12: Exploring Different Freelance Writing Types — 103

Chapter 13: Common Spelling and Grammar Mistakes that Freelance Writers Make — 109

Chapter 14: From Beginner to Expert: The Freelance Flywheel — 117

Chapter 15: Your Post-Project Checklist — 123

✴ **Part 2: The Business Fundamentals of Freelancing** — 127

Chapter 16: "Business School" for Freelancers — 131

Chapter 17: Crafting Your Freelance Writing Agreement — 137

Chapter 18: The Art of Negotiation — 143

✳ Part 3: How to Land Better, Higher-Paying Clients 149

Chapter 19: Where Are All the High-Paying Clients? 155

Chapter 20: From Day Job to Full-Time Freelance Writer 163

Chapter 21: Automating Your Client Workflow 169

Chapter 22: Hire and Work with a Virtual Assistant 175

Chapter 23: Building a Freelancing Agency 185

Chapter 24: How to Level Up Your Writing Skill 191

Chapter 25: Value-Based Pricing and Packages 201

✳ Part 4: Building Your Ideal Life as a Freelance Writer 207

Chapter 26: Using Mindset Shifts to Make Your Ideal Life a Reality 211

Chapter 27: Preventing Burnout as a Freelance Writer 219

Chapter 28: Freelancing with a Chronic Illness 229

Chapter 29: The Year-Long Freelance Roadmap and Opportunity Calendar 235

Chapter 30: Building Passive Income 239

Chapter 31: What to Do When Work Slows Down 243

Chapter 32: Leveraging Success as a Freelancer 253

Chapter 33: The Never-Ending Chapter 259

✳ Acknowledgments 261
✳ About the Author 261

INTRODUCTION
WHY MOST PEOPLE FAIL AT FREELANCING

It was the Fourth of July during the 2020 pandemic, and I was depressed and stress eating bread alone in the dark—a classic coping strategy. I was sitting on my tiny, beat-up loveseat I had dragged over from my previous Los Angeles apartment, watching episodes of ABC's *Shark Tank*, where eager founders pitch investors with hopes of getting their business funded.

I watched as the entrepreneurs pitched the Sharks: this episode's parade of founders had "figured it out"—or, had bet their mortgage on their business that mailed literal potatoes to customers with messages on them (which ended up being more lucrative than you'd think.) All of the contestants were on that stage in the hopes they, too, could achieve their version of the lucrative "American Dream."

At the time, my freelance writing business had been hit by the shock of the pandemic shutdowns. My early twenties were spent working a string of minimum-wage jobs, and I had left everything behind to go full-time freelance.

Am I stupid for trying to make it on my own? I thought in the dark as the fireworks exploded above me. *Do I just need a steady job to wait out the pandemic?*

In the dark of my living room, I hoped I could figure out this whole freelance thing. More than that: I *needed* to make it work if I wanted to have any hopes of paying my bills without resorting to gluing postage stamps to produce.

Fast-forward to two years later: I had just returned from a trip to Portugal—one of my favorite countries I'd visited so far in my travels—and I was about to hit my first $50,000 *month* as a freelancer.

"No way." I couldn't believe it: each month I had broken records, consistently earning $30,000 on average *per month* as a freelance writer. Hadn't the world told me by now that this should be impossible? Weren't writers supposed to starve and live off coffee and cigarettes?

But there it was: $50,000 in revenue for my freelancing business that month. I felt an unfathomable high as I crunched the numbers from the kitchen table. Even if everything disappeared tomorrow, I could say that *I made it*. That capitalist "American Dream" wasn't reserved for someone who made it big by writing personalized messages on potatoes on *Shark Tank*.

To me, those numbers meant I could pay for my expensive $800/month (after insurance) medication for my autoimmune condition. Those numbers meant I could continue to travel the world and make my own schedule—no alarm clock for me. Those numbers meant I could be more generous with those I loved. Those numbers meant I could continue to invest in making art with my peers.

Those numbers meant I could live my dream life, no strings attached.

Why Full-Time Jobs are a Scam

If you're considering going freelance—or maybe you're a newly minted freelance writer!—you might be dealing with that crippling fear we all deal with when going against the grain. I'm sure you've heard jokes that "freelancing" is just a fancy word for "unemployed." You've probably garnered worry from friends and family that are skeptical of your ability to make any money whatsoever, or assume you're moonlighting as a rideshare driver or grocery delivery person to actually make ends meet.

In reality, financial freedom and time abundance is within reach as a freelancer—less so if you're an employee. Here's why: employees don't often get to participate in profits of the business you're working for. You get a paycheck—maybe a bonus or sometimes shares in the company—but it's in your employer's interest to keep your wages as low as you'll accept. You can be a top performer but still face layoffs and job insecurity because all your eggs are in one basket.

Society wants you to stay an employee: you've been programmed since the day you stepped foot in school to be an "A-Student." Show up on time, work your forty, fifty, sixty, or 120 hours per week (especially if you want that raise), and when you're sixty-five you might be able to retire. But that's only if you avoid layoffs, inflation, bad investments, and catastrophic medical bills. Not to mention, you're probably working for the "C-Students" and dropouts instead of leveraging your own skills and specific knowledge to make a living.

The freelancers who have used my tools have gone on to find financial freedom and success *without* having to trade the best days/years/decades of their life working for others in order to afford retirement down the road. The people who use my strategies unlock the ability to travel the world, wake up whenever they want, and spend their days wherever and however they choose. As I write this section, it's an unusually warm Tuesday in London and I just strolled down the historic Brick Lane neighborhood to pick up a matcha latte before settling into my work at around 11am. The freelance life affords many little luxuries most people can only dream of.

Freelancers also have the opportunity to work with incredible people. My clients are top investors, founders, and pro athletes. I've written for companies valued at over a billion dollars, and I've been flown out to work with some of the most fascinating people in the world.

Instead of signing your years away to work hard at a company for someone else to get rich, why not make a name for yourself and leverage your own talents? Unlike an employee, freelancers have an unparalleled bargaining power. You can raise your rates whenever you want, and as you increase client demand for your services and learn how to provide extraordinary value, you'll find that people won't pass up the chance to work with you, no matter the cost.

Why Most Freelancers Fail at Building Six-Figure Careers

Most freelancers fail because they don't understand the strategy of how to build a six-figure freelancing career. If they knew what I'm about to share with you in this book, they would realize that there are so many clients clamoring to work with talented and reliable freelancers—and they'll pay top dollar for your skills, too. This is especially true for post-pandemic remote work, which has ushered in a golden era of freelancing.

There's this myth that freelance writers are on-demand labor who struggle at the hands of the "gig economy." But that couldn't be further from the truth, as freelancing is an economy of artisan talent. You can build a career where you're a respected craftsman with plenty of time (and money!) to pursue your own art, travel the world, and live well. I've coined the term "Artisan Freelancer" to refer to freelance writers and creatives who utilize their skills and artistry to craft an extraordinary life for themselves—while still pursuing their own passion projects and interests. Anyone can be an Artisan Freelancer if they employ the strategies in this book to work smarter and get paid well for their time.

It was only when I sat down to write this book that I finally was able to codify the strategy that took me from $4,000/month to $6,000/month in 2020 as a freelancer writer to $50,000 months in 2022 working roughly fifteen to twenty hours per week.

In short? Better clients, higher rates, thoughtful systems, a specific niche, clever sales letters, and above all else, a new mindset, holistic habits, and a feverish protection of my free time. All of that ensured that I would never work sixty- to eighty-hour weeks ever again.

Don't worry, I'll walk you through all of these core strategies step-by-step in the coming chapters so you can carve out your own unique path to a life worth living.

Why My Strategy Works for Freelance Writers

The title of this book is *Six-Figure Freelance Writer*. I know there are plenty of other books that say similar things, but I wanted to add a focus to this book that I saw that all the others ignored, which is why I included: *A Holistic Guide to Finding Freedom in Freelancing*. That's the secret ingredient that was missing from this sauce before I was making astronomical numbers in my own freelance writing business and found the "stability" I was craving.

Making six figures as a freelancer is more than just selling clients on your services. It's about all of the other pieces of your life, the pieces that inform how you approach the work, what you specialize in, and how rested and happy you are.

By optimizing for a fulfilled, happy, stress-free life—which I was forced to do after developing a chronic illness triggered by workaholism—

INTRODUCTION

you unlock a level of health, wealth, and success that's only available to those who address their root mindset and habits. I don't want you to wait until you have to make a change, I want you to choose to change. Trust me: it's better that way.

Hustle culture is a thing of the past: this book isn't about dishing out productivity hacks or stuffing your calendar with constant meetings. It's about learning how to work smarter, not harder. I cover how to price out packages and your hourly rate in a way that will provide value to your clients so you can spend less time selling and more time doing whatever you want.

A Note on Footnotes and Free Digital Resources

I've scattered free digital resources for you across this book. Anytime you see the footnote icon[1] you can find a link to either a webpage with more resources, or another note I may have for you.

I've included hundreds of dollars' worth of resources in this book for you, which I'm giving away to you for the price of this book. Why? Because good things come to those who read.

Why I'm Sharing My Secrets With You

I'm writing this book because it's the advice I wish I had gotten. Sometimes, people ask me why I'm giving out all my tips and tricks—down to the exact proposal letter I use to land my $50,000+ projects and clients. Why would I share this stuff with you, my competition?

Honestly, I'd love for you to take my clients. I get far too many incoming client requests than I know what to do with, and I have no desire to start a traditional agency (*woof...* more on that, later) or scale too much further than where I'm at now. I know that the market for freelancers is only going to grow as companies get more comfortable with remote work and freelance talent, so there's plenty of room for all of us. Not every client is going to love every freelancer, so it's better for the marketplace if there's more talent to help fill the demand.

I also got to where I am because of the great advice I received along

---

1   Hello! Welcome to a footnote. Happy treasure hunting!

the way, so I feel a sense of duty to pay it forward. My life now affords me time to pursue my creative passions, heal my body, travel the world, and do meaningful work with awesome clients—and I believe everyone should be able to do the same.

Whether you're a digital nomad, a new freelance writer looking to quit your day job, or a veteran freelance writer ready to level up your skills and pricing structure—

This book is for _you_.

It's written with all the love and care I could give because you deserve the best advice to create your dream life.

So, welcome. Welcome to the future of work, where we all love what we do every day and can participate in the creative economy and lend our talents in ways that provide for meaningful and fulfilling lives.

The only question you have to answer is: are you ready to hit your first six-figure year?

PART I

GETTING STARTED AS A FREELANCE WRITER

PART I: GETTING STARTED AS A FREELANCE WRITER

STORY #1:
DISPATCHES FROM A FREELANCE WRITER'S LIFE

From Venice, California to Venice, Italy

It was fall of 2017 and I decided I couldn't do my best work in my tiny studio apartment I shared with my cat in west Los Angeles. My apartment had no natural light: the only window faced a wall, and my cat and I shared a few hundred square feet of space. Me-*ow* is right.

I was in a weird place in my life: I was using freelancing as a placeholder until I found a better, happier job in Hollywood (which I would later realize was a contradiction!) I wanted to be a TV writer, spending my days in writers' rooms daydreaming in fiction. Little did I know that what I really wanted (travel, time to pursue my art, financial security) would come from my freelance career, not from a job in Hollywood. But, if I wanted to try my hand at this freelancing stuff, I decided that I needed a space to do so.

I ventured out of my tiny studio and started to spend my days writing in a co-working space near Venice. *I'll be more motivated this way*, I thought to myself as I tried to justify the hefty signup fee for the space.

As I settled into a trendy desk at the co-working space with a glass of lemon water by my side, I opened my laptop and started tinkering on my portfolio. *If I'm going to afford my life here in LA, I need to earn more*, I told myself. And then, with a shaky hand, I raised my rates to $35/hour on my freelancing profile.

The intrusive thoughts flooded into my brain: *Will someone pay that? That's more than double what I'm making as an assistant! Is this possi-*

ble? Is karma going to hunt me down and frame me for the highest level of white-collar espionage?

As the whispers flew around my mind like the ghosts of film school past, I sent them away with a single click: *submit*.

Fast-forward to 2021. I had just raised my rates again, this time adding a zero: $350/hour. I was lounging in a hostel room in Venice, Italy, and our room overlooked the Venice canals. The restored building bled with character: murals on the ceiling, original architecture, and courtyards humming with late-night conversation over glasses of wine as tourists and students alike flocked to the floating city.

My partner Kyle and I spent our days in Venice protecting our crepes from hungry seagulls and sightseeing in the sinking city. Our three months working remotely in Europe and twelve months of working remotely in the U.S. was coming to a brief hiatus as the holidays approached.

While traveling, I often work out of a co-working space, and we worked in a number of different co-working spaces in Italy. *It will be better to separate our home life in our loft from our work space*, we had decided since both Kyle and I also needed spaces for our Zoom calls during the two days per week we did meetings. After we finished our work for the day, we'd stroll the cobblestone streets and eat the best pizza you can imagine.

While my life wasn't spent in writers' rooms in Hollywood, I was still writing plenty: Kyle and I had written and produced several scripted podcasts, and I was embarking on a novel that I had been itching to write for years.

There was one huge career change that took me from barely making it in a cramped studio apartment to flourishing as a writer in the streets of European cities. That magic ingredient?

It wasn't writing for Hollywood or getting an agent. The secret was going all in on freelance writing. And no, you don't need a co-working membership to get started—just a dream of a better life and a plan on how to get there. And you don't have to figure it out from scratch: I'm here to help.

Let's get started!

PART I: GETTING STARTED AS A FREELANCE WRITER

CHAPTER 1:
CHECKLIST FOR NEW FREELANCE WRITERS

"Yeah, yeah, freelancing is great—but where do I start?"

I answer all questions like this with my favorite tool: a checklist.

Getting started as a freelance writer can feel a bit overwhelming, so I created this foundational checklist you can hang on your fridge and check off as you go.

Don't fret if it seems like a lot: we will cover everything in future chapters!

Checklist for New Freelance Writers:

- Write your bio
- Take your headshot
- Set your hourly rate
- Pick your niche
- Learn more about your craft
- Write your proposal cover letters/cold email templates
- Pick a freelancing platform and submit proposals daily
- Create a vision board for your ideal future (old-school magazine collages or detective-style corkboards complete with red-string are highly recommended)
- Learn how to create a daily success routine and optimize your habits using tried-and-true tricks
- Plan your stress reduction tactics

Checklist for Expert Freelance Writers:

- Start a website with a blog and optimize your keywords so your clients can find you
- Optimize your social media so your clients can find you
- Create your outreach strategy to reach clients outside of freelance platforms
- Set your package rates
- Create your client workflow, with the help of automations
- Hire an accountant to help with taxes and/or bookkeeping
- Purchase a health insurance policy (either through your state's marketplace or with the help of a health insurance broker), and set up a health savings account (HSA) if you have a high deductible health plan (depending on what your CPA recommends!)
- Save for retirement and set up a Roth IRA (or whatever your CPA recommends! You'll hear this a lot)
- Hire a lawyer to help you create contract templates
- Purchase professional liability insurance
- Learn how to assemble a team and outsource when you need help
- Continue learning more about your ideal client and how to market to them

And that's it for now! Once you've checked off most of the basics, the later chapters in this book will help you continue to hone your craft on your journey to becoming an expert freelancer.

PART I: GETTING STARTED AS A FREELANCE WRITER

CHAPTER 2:
PICKING A FREELANCE WRITING NICHE

When you're getting started as a freelance writer, you probably aren't thinking about specializing. "I can do it all!" you might say as you pound espresso shots from your local coffee shop.

To that, I say: "but why would you want to?"

Before you protest, I'm a fellow multi-passionate person. My list of hobbies runs longer than a CVS receipt. I love doing it all. But when it comes to freelance writing, I realized the moment I specialized and narrowed my focus, the more opportunities started flowing my way. And I didn't even have to specialize as narrowly as you're probably thinking.

The key here? To find an obsession that will become your secret weapon.

From a Lamp to a Laser: Finding Focus for Success

When I started as a freelance writer, I applied for every job that I thought I could do on freelance platforms. I wrote everything from art magazine pieces to pitch deck copy. I didn't brand myself as one type of writer: I did it all. I liked the variety, and each time I landed a new type of assignment, I felt giddy with excitement.

But the constant stream of new types of assignments started to wear on me in year two of my part-time freelancing journey. I felt like I was too scattered: I didn't have any consistency, and I was always having to generate new quotes and prices for projects. I couldn't standardize any of my systems because I had no "standard" work.

And then, I stumbled upon memoir ghostwriting and fell in love.

Memoir ghostwriting became my first serious niche. In order to attract clients, I wrote an article on my website about my approach. I started writing samples for my portfolio about my own life in an autobiographical style to show off my prose, and started zeroing in on potential memoir clients on freelance platforms.

I was still writing blog posts and webpages and all the random assignments that came my way, but now I had a focus and a steady flow of work from people who saw me as an expert at memoir ghostwriting—because I became one!

I read memoirs day in and day out, and spent hours on calls with clients hearing about their life stories. I helped NBA players, Silicon Valley CEOs, and innocent victims of foreign justice systems. I wrote redemption stories, family stories, and coming-of-age stories. My clients flew me out to interview them, and for the first time, I saw how being an expert paid off.

As a freelance writer, you have to go from **being a lamp** to **being a laser**: direct your focus to one niche that you love.

Why (and How!) Experts Win

So why do most freelance writers who don't specialize in a niche often lose out on jobs to freelancers who do?

The reality is people like to hire experts: they don't want a writer who can do a bunch of things well, they want the *best* writer that can do the one thing for their project. Bruce Lee didn't fear the person who knew a thousand punches. He feared the person who practiced one punch a thousand times. Strike the fear of how much worse a client's projects will be without the special flick of your wrist.

I've seen writers specialize in things as specific as "construction copywriting" or "skincare blogging" who get a ton of work, so pick a niche and learn how to develop a deep portfolio around that niche. It may seem counterintuitive at first, but being as focused as possible will get you more work than you'd even know what to do with. That's because clients want to work with experts, so while your niche can change, it's important to understand how you can become an expert for realtors listing properties in the metaverse.

Trust me: you'll be rewarded handsomely for finding your focus.

What If I Don't Know What My Niche Should Be?

What are you obsessed with? This is the question that should guide your initial search on finding a niche.

Your niche should be an area you love writing in. It should be something you're curious about and want to hone your skills and learn more about! The goal here is to pick a type of work that feels like play. Even though there may be days when you're burned out or tired, you should feel a flutter of excitement when you're thinking about your chosen niche.

As a memoir ghostwriter, I'm a bit nosy by nature. I love to hear about people's lives, their high school crushes, their deepest darkest secrets they won't share with anyone else. I'm ready to hear them spill the tea on a video call or over voice memos, and my curiosity makes the work fun for both myself and my client.

You don't have to secretly love drama like I do to be good at this work: you could also be a therapist with the same interest (they're often freelancers, too!). You just need to find the intersection of what you love and what the world needs (and will pay you for!) So, while "newspaper advertisement writer" might have been bangin' bucks back in the day, you're probably better off specializing in writing Internet ad copy these days.

Keep looking until you find your perfect niche and don't be afraid to learn new skills if you need to spend some time exploring!

✷ Quick Tip: Learn from Fellow Freelancers

Want a quick way to see what's working for other writers? Just browse LinkedIn or freelance platforms like Upwork and see what other freelance writers are doing (and what they're earning!) and use this as your own personal market research into what niches people are writing and loving. Freelancing isn't a competition, but it helps to know what other writers are charging and making so you can understand what potential clients are paying for and find value in.

Can I Have Multiple Freelance Writing Niches?

"But Amy, you're both a memoir ghostwriter and a tech copywriter? Aren't those multiple niches?"

Yes, but let me break it down. When my freelancing began taking off, my **primary** focus was a memoir ghostwriter with a **secondary** focus on copywriting for tech companies. When web3 started taking off and NFT collections were in need of storytelling, I switched my primary focus to web3 copywriting and storytelling with memoirs as my secondary focus.

I do this by having different "landing pages" for different clients. Most of my memoir clients find me through a blog post I wrote about how to hire a ghostwriter to write your memoir that ranks on Google. They don't know me as a tech copywriter, just an expert ghostwriter. Same thing for my copywriting clients: they find me through my profiles, website, and cold emails. They may not know that I also do memoir ghostwriting.

So yes, you can have two different niches, but one needs to be the focus (and should be emphasized in your online presence!) Build up one niche and knock it out of the park, and only then can you start to explore adding on additional interests and niches. Always focus on pursuing mastery first.

When to Pivot to a Different Niche

Here's a great rule to live by: if you're feeling burned out and bored and rest isn't helping, it's time to mix things up.

I like to call this ***intuitive work***. If your intuition is like, "hey, I don't really want to hear about someone's childhood trauma this month" then maybe turning down that new memoir and instead learning more about how to be a freelance travel blogger is the way to go.

Alternatively, you might realize that a new technology or trend is about to start a huge new wave of innovation, and you want to work in a new sector or industry to be a part of that.

That's the nice thing about freelance work: you don't have a boss forcing you to do something. The only rules are the ones you collaboratively decide on with your client and put into a contract.

The rest is up to you. So, pivot to your heart's desire—as long as you're not using "pivoting" as an excuse to avoid hard work.

Thinking About Niches: the Duck vs. the Cheetah

Cheetahs and ducks survive in the wild for very different reasons. Cheetahs are great at one thing: they're super fast. But what about ducks? They're pretty good at flying, walking, and swimming, but won't be winning a 5k anytime soon.

As a freelance writer, I see lots of freelancers with hyper-specific niches make bank. Their marketing looks like: "as a copywriter, I optimize email marketing copy for electric vehicles" or "I ghostwrite memoirs for famous Internet personalities."

These people are cheetahs. They're the best in one specific area. *Rawr.*

This type of specialization works because people pay top dollar for specialists. If you own an antique car, you're going to hire a mechanic who has experience servicing that type of car because you want the best of *the best* for *your* best.

But you don't have to be a hardcore specialist. I'm not: I specialized in one thing and then added a secondary specialization soon after. I stacked my skills on top of each other, and pursued mastery one niche at a time.

Think of the handyman who comes to your house and not only fixes your leaky sink, but helps to re-hang a crooked TV. Having a professional who is highly skilled at a number of related tasks comes in handy when you're not wanting to hire five different handymen when you could have just hired one. This is a practice known as *skill stacking*: combining multiple skills in order to provide a more valuable service or set of services. This is what I do, and I find it works well for me and keeps me interested in the work.

Now, there are pros and cons to being a cheetah or a duck. Specialization can get boring, and you might have a smaller client base. But if you pick the right niche, you're set for life.

Being a Swiss army knife can be more fun, but you also have to devote more time to learning new things, fast.

If you love systematizing your work and don't like learning new things, find a lucrative niche to specialize in. If you love learning and are a fast and thorough researcher, be a Swiss army knife. Learn how to solve your clients' problems across a number of written deliverables.

Mastery First, Then Exploration

I've always taken writing seriously as a craft. I started with angsty poetry and navel-gazing short stories until I found my way to novel writing. I wrote a novel every year during National Novel Writing Month starting from the time I was fourteen until I turned nineteen. I also wrote screenplays and blog posts, and wrote and produced my own content during my undergrad at USC in their screenwriting program.

My focus with everything I wrote was to gain experience so I could master my craft. I knew that I wouldn't be able to hit perfection right off the bat: I needed to try out different forms and styles and practice the fundamentals until I could get to where I wanted to be.

You don't have to have as much writing experience as I do to be a successful freelance writer, but you do need to pursue mastery in your chosen niche before you can move onto a new niche. You'll hurt your career if you split your focus before you've truly mastered the niche you're in to go jump for the next shiny opportunity.

So, the moment the shoe fits, it's time to dance all night and kiss a few princes so you can really break in your sick new footwear. Only after taking your niche for a spin can you determine if it's a keeper, or if you need to call up your fairy godmother for some new glass footwear.

Which Niche Makes the Most Money?

Want to know what niche is the most profitable? It's the one that intersects with an in-demand industry and what you love to write.

If you chase a type of freelance writing *only* because it pays the big bucks, you'll burn out more quickly and won't be able to compete against other freelancers who actually love these types of copywriting formats. You might hate writing whitepapers, and that's okay! Don't do them. The key is to find the thing you like to do with the person who'd like you to do it.

However, if your brain gets really excited when you're visualizing new ways of telling a story through an animated explainer video, or you love the creative constraints of a webpage—amazing! That's the type of work you should lean into.

Any type of writing that helps drive a sale and market a product or service will naturally be in higher demand. However, if you love something

PART 1: GETTING STARTED AS A FREELANCE WRITER

like memoir ghostwriting, you can still reach your six-figure income goals as long as you're differentiating yourself from the competition by figuring out what unique perspective or framework you're offering.

What if I Don't Know What I Want to Specialize In?

Then it's time to book a one-way flight to Thailand or another relatively cheap tropical country and figure out what your true passions are. Become a digital nomad, sell all of your possessions, and reduce your overhead so you can have time and energy to find yourself and wander back to the path you're meant to be on.

This is what I did: I sold everything I owned and hit the road. I'm still a digital nomad as of the writing of this book. I love the freedom that comes with travel, and my overhead is so low. I don't own anything except for what's in my suitcase, and my monthly spend is much lower than when I was a full-time city dweller buying $25 cocktails at overpriced bars.

If you need time, make time. If you need space, make space. If you need freedom, find a way to get free. You might need to make sacrifices, but the road will be better when you can pave it with passion.

As you make more space in your life, increase your number of inputs. Meet new people, read new books, and explore the world. Let your curiosity guide you to a better tomorrow.

Amy's Field Notes: A Moment of Clarity in Florence, Italy

A pivotal point in my freelance business happened when my partner Kyle and I were walking around Florence, Italy.

I had just gotten off a great call with a new tech client, but the rest of my freelance work was not going as swimmingly.

"I feel so burned out all the time," I complained to Kyle as we walked in circles around *Piazza della Indipendenza*. I sipped an espresso to-go in a paper cup (yes, this is a travesty in Italy, I know) while Kyle licked his gelato (less of a travesty than my to-go cup, but walking-and-eating is still frowned upon in slower-paced European countries.) Filthy Americans we are.

"This espresso better fix all my problems," I grumbled.

"What specifically is burning you out?" Kyle asked in the pensive, wise way he always did when he was about to swoop in and help me solve a problem.

"These tiny, one-off projects. Like the bio I wrote for that guy when we were staying in Milan."

"Yeah, he was not a good client to work with," Kyle said.

"And I didn't even realize that article I agreed to write was a college essay until I started the job," I said.

"No more writing rich kids' essays," Kyle replied.

"I couldn't help it, I was bamboozled," I said.

"But what do you like working on right now?"

We walked in silence for a moment. Kids were running around despite it being late at night: all of Italy felt like a country of night owls. The buildings around us were lit by the warm street lights, and the end-of-summer breeze was just starting to turn cool. I contemplated my projects, the things that were bringing me life, and the things that I was dreading that had driven me to drink espresso at 10pm to prepare for my night of rewrites.

"Honestly? I love the new tech jobs I've been doing. The clients are professional, the copywriting feels natural and fun to me, and it's a challenge I've always enjoyed."

"Great," Kyle said, "then just focus on that, and drop the rest. And no more small jobs under $3,000."

After that conversation, I stopped being an inch deep and a mile wide. Instead, I zeroed in on the mile deep and an inch wide, and struck gold soon after.

You might not have a Kyle in your life, so let me be that voice in your head that asks, "what's going right? What do you want more of? Focus on that. What do you need less of? Cut that."

PART I: GETTING STARTED AS A FREELANCE WRITER

CHAPTER 3:
BUILDING YOUR BIO AND TAKING YOUR HEADSHOT

Before you run screaming to the hills, I want you to know that building a "personal brand" is part of the deal of being a freelance writer (and it's not as daunting as you think!)

Listen, I know that upon first glance the whole concept of a "personal brand" feels like a capitalist play to auction off your time to the machine of the gig economy. This is a common criticism in response to those building their solopreneur business, so it's best to just ignore the critics in the stands and focus on your job in the ring.

In reality, a personal brand is just your reputation online:

- What do you do?
- What do people associate you with?
- What kinds of services can they hire you for?
- Can they even find you online if they want to hire you?

All of that starts and ends with your personal branding, and that begins with the foundation of your bio and headshot.

In an equitable world, your headshot wouldn't matter. Great writing would speak for itself, and your appearance wouldn't affect that. However, we're not in an equitable world, and people love to visualize who they're working with, both on your freelance portfolio and on video calls.

So, while we're on our way to build a more equitable world, I'll provide some tips to make sure you come across as friendly and experienced in both your headshot and bio.

How to Take a Great Headshot

Headshots are important, and they should give potential clients a feel of who you are and what your vibe is.

I don't usually smile in my photos because I'm a stone-cold killer and they should expect that from me. (Okay, so in reality I'm just bad at smiling authentically on-command.) But I smile in my headshot because my clients aren't hiring a stone-cold killer (at least not on freelance platforms), and they want to know they're getting into business with a freelancer who will be friendly and easy to work with.

If you feel like your headshot isn't representative of you, try enlisting a friend or family member and take a super simple photo that's inside a well-lit area, or outside at the park or by the beach. Make sure your background isn't distracting: solid colors or simple landscapes are best.

You don't even need a professional photographer, just nice natural lighting and a smile! Don't wear patterns that are too distracting unless you're a comedy writer and that's your #Brand.

If you've been freelancing for a while and can hire a professional photographer to take your photo, I would recommend it. Remember, high-end clients want to work with high-end freelancers, so if you're at the stage in your career where you're leveling up, make sure to redo your marketing materials to reflect what your ideal clients want to see.

✹ Quick Tip: Build a High-End Personal Brand

When putting together your initial marketing materials, think about how you want to be perceived. What colors represent your services? Are you trying to evoke a bright, cheerfulness? Or a cool calm? Match your personal brand with your personality to stay authentic to yourself. I leaned into neutrals with pops of pastels and cursive text. I picked a lavender background for my headshot. I wanted to give my materials a feminine touch, but still stay minimalist. Understand what feelings you want to evoke in your ideal client when you're picking out your headshot and setting up your first set of materials. Don't overthink it: you can always rebrand later.

How to Write a Killer Bio for Your Writing Niche

"So, what do you do? And how can you help me?"

Your bio should answer both of these questions by covering your experience and focus. Your bio needs to be persuasive, explaining exactly why you're the best at what you do—and how you can provide value for potential clients.

Here are my top tips for writing a bio that kicks off a great first impression:

- **Get specific about relevant experience that sets you apart.** This isn't a resume, so don't include every job you've ever had, just the experiences that will make a potential client nod their head and say, "ah yes, we've found the writer who can save us! The prophecy has come true!"

- **Try and imbue your bio with voice and confidence.** By "voice" I mean make your bio sound like you–don't just rattle off jokes or try to be witty (unless that's your schtick.) Write with confidence: use sentences that hit hard and cut unnecessary words and transitions.

- **Think about impact: what is the most important thing for the reader to take away from your bio?** What should they know about you after reading? What feeling do you want them to have? Then, pressure test each sentence to see if it achieves just that. Cut the fat until you have the cleanest, most precise bio money could only hope to buy.

Anatomy of a Bio

Because I think writing anything is better with a template, I'm including the "template" of how I think a great bio should be written.

As of the writing of this book, here's my current bio that I use for my focus in the memoir ghostwriting niche:

Amy Suto began her career as a Hollywood TV writer before hitting the road and becoming a digital nomad and six-figure freelance writer. She specializes in serving clients as a memoir ghostwriter and writes books for professional athletes, Silicon Valley CEOs, and other inspiring individuals. Amy taps into her seven years of professional storytelling experience to help her clients become bestselling authors and TED speakers. When she's not writing, Amy travels the world and works remotely from cafes in Prague—or is misplacing her AirPods in Lisbon. You can learn more about Amy at: AmySuto.com.

Because your bio is your ultimate "sales" tool, there should be some serious thought and psychology that goes into how you write it, so I'll share how I went about crafting mine.

As you read the next section, just remember: a bio is just five or six sentences that convey all the information a potential client would want to know about you. I'll walk you through each section step-by-step:

Always start with a sentence sharing where you've been and any **relevant background experience**:

Amy Suto began her career as a Hollywood TV writer before hitting the road and becoming a digital nomad and six-figure freelance writer.

Also, note that I used my first and last name. Some new freelancers just use their first name, but remember that you're building a personal brand: you want people to recognize who you are. You're not just "Bond." You're *James* Bond, duh. So, make sure the people know your full name before you beat them senseless in an Eastern European bathroom—*er,*

PART I: GETTING STARTED AS A FREELANCE WRITER

write incredible copy for them.

Next, indicate your **expertise and niche**:

She specializes in serving clients as a memoir ghostwriter and writes books for professional athletes, Silicon Valley CEOs, and other inspiring individuals.

If you have any keywords you're targeting (like "memoir ghostwriter") make sure they're written out in the way that clients will search for them. Optimizing your bio for search engines as well as humans is a true black-belt move that will make Google and other sly search engines like LinkedIn your best friends.

Your niche is then followed by your **secret sauce** (aka your USP or unique selling proposal):

Amy taps into her seven years of professional storytelling experience to help her clients become bestselling authors and TED speakers.

This section is where you should sell yourself and your experiences. What makes you different than your competition? And, more importantly, how does that impact your clients and the outcome of the work you do for them?

And then, share a bit about yourself like a fun fact or something cool that you're doing:

When she's not writing, Amy travels the world and works remotely from cafes in Prague—or is misplacing her AirPods in Lisbon.

I like making fun facts location-based so people can get a sense of what time zone you're usually in, or, if you're a digital nomad like me, they can expect you to be a more asynchronous partner-in-crime. I'm also singlehandedly keeping Apple's AirPods revenue at record highs by always misplacing mine. You're welcome, Apple.

Last but not least, include your **call-to-action** (CTA) sharing where clients can learn more about you:

You can learn more about Amy at: AmySuto.com.

Always have a call-to-action that sends people to a website where they can enter their email address and get added to a newsletter. While your services might not be a right fit for them today, you want to stay in touch and cultivate your leads if that changes in the future.

Last Words on First Impressions

Your bio should be a living, breathing document that evolves to fit your experiences, niche, and where you're headed. Be sure to revisit your bio every so often to make sure it still rings true to you and your writing journey!

Amy's Field Notes: How I Rebranded and Became a "Luxury" Freelancer

My partner Kyle had a good challenge for me: "how can you turn your service into a luxury good?" he asked. "What would make you the Louis Vuitton of freelance writers?"

So, I thought about it. Up until that point, I had been pretty scrappy with building my brand. I built my own website, designed my own graphics—I did everything myself. My materials weren't cheap, per se, but they didn't feel high-end, either.

This was a pivotal moment: before my rebrand of all of my materials, I had capped out at a few thousand dollars per month as a freelancer. I had trouble surpassing $8,000 months, and was struggling to acquire as many new clients as I wanted to. So, I decided to move forward with my rebrand.

I hired a website designer for about $4,000 to build a new website from scratch, and move over almost one hundred of my old blog posts. They wrote over one hundred custom lines of code for me, and I spent months redesigning every inch of my new website. The final product is still live on my site AmySuto.com, and I still get compliments on it to this day.

I didn't stop there: I hired a professional headshot photographer, and also did a photo session in a loft I rented so I had cohesive photos similar to my brand that I could post. I use all of these photos to this day, and am planning another photoshoot soon. I spent around $1,000 on this suite of photos, from the headshots to over one hundred "lifestyle" images shot on film and digitally that I use in all my sales materials.

I'm not going to lie—it was nerve-wracking to spend this much on my own materials. I'm a freelancer after all: I know the value of a dollar and it's tough to part with hard-earned cash not knowing what the end results would be.

So, was this rebrand a waste of money? I'll let you be the judge.

After my rebrand and all of these materials went live, I went from being unable to surpass $8,000 per month to growing gradually each month to now (over a year later in 2022) booking over $50,000 per month.

The $5,000 I spent on my rebrand was a drop in the bucket compared to the shift that happened when my clients started perceiving me as a high-end professional. I wasn't just a girl using a stock WordPress template. I was an expert, with the branding to back it up.
But what changed?

I had put a level of detail and thoughtfulness into my materials that showed my clients how meticulous I was. They felt confident taking a risk on me because they saw how great my materials were, and trusted me.

I'm not recommending new freelancers go out and spend what I did right out of the gate. I spent next to $0 on my materials as a new freelancer. But once you start hitting a ceiling, it may be time to hire professional help to bring your brand to the next level.

CHAPTER 4:
CALCULATING YOUR HOURLY RATE

Your hourly rate is the basis of *all* your pricing. Your hourly rate shows you what you need to charge for fixed-rate assignments and it helps you decide whether or not a project is worth taking.

Your rate needs to encapsulate all of the expenses that come with freelancing: remember, your clients are getting access to your talent on-demand, and you're covering the costs employers usually cover (such as health insurance, retirement, a great selection of coffee and tea in your kitchen, ping-pong tables for your home office, and other mission-critical benefits.) This means your hourly rate as a freelancer will be much higher than if you were an employee because of these added costs.

If you're ready to calculate your target hourly rate, below are some common expenses (both personal and business-related!) for you to think about.

All right, get your calculators out!

NOTE: None of this is financial advice, so be sure to talk to an accountant before you begin freelancing and making financial decisions.

Let's begin![2]

---

[2] Want to access a downloadable copy of this worksheet? Visit: <u>amysuto.com/six-figure-freelancer</u>

Monthly Personal Expenses Calculator

What are your monthly living expenses? Divide any annual costs into monthly chunks for accuracy.

In calculating your monthly expenses, consider:

Rent/mortgage/property taxes:	
Car payment/car insurance/gas:	
Food (groceries and dining out):	
Utilities:	
Subscriptions:	
Entertainment:	
Travel:	
Shopping:	
Monthly debt payments/loans/etc:	
Savings for Health Savings Account (HSA)/ retirement accounts such as a Roth IRA/ your emergency fund:	
Other:	
SUBTOTAL PERSONAL EXPENSES :	

Monthly Business Expense Calculator

Some of these business expenses may be new to you if you're going full-time freelance.

Here they are:

Health insurance:	
Bookkeeping software/accountant and/or bookkeeper fees:	
General liability insurance:	
Marketing fees for your services:	
Domain hosting fees for your website:	
Legal fees for creation and setup of your corporation/LLC and contracts:	
Business software subscriptions:	
Writer's assistant/proofreader fees:	
Computer/home office equipment/furniture:	
State taxes for your entity (i.e., as of the writing of this book, CA has an $800 annual franchise tax for entities like LLCs):	
SUBTOTAL BUSINESS EXPENSES :	

Calculate Your Hourly Rate

Now, take the **number of hours you want to work each week (H)** and subtract the **number of hours you'll probably spend on admin work (A)** (i.e., the unpaid hours you spend sending cold emails or proposals, messaging clients, potential client calls, marketing your services)

(H)-(A) = Number of Hours You Have Available for Billable Work (B)

EXAMPLE: I'll go ahead and say I want to work 20 hours per week and spend 5 hours per week doing admin work. I only have 15 hours per week available for billable work (B).

From there, take your monthly expenses and divide it by your hours available for billable work **(B)**:

Monthly Personal + Biz Expenses / (B) x 4 = HOURLY RATE

EXAMPLE: I'll say I have $7,000 of monthly expenses and divide that by the number of hours I have available for billable work (B=15) multiplied by 4 (the number of estimated weeks in a month).

So:

$7,000 divided by 60 gives me: 116

That means my hourly rate is: **~$116 per hour at 15 billable hours per week, and 20 total hours worked per week.**

Does That Rate Seem High? Don't Panic!

This is where things like fixed-rate projects come in. Ideally, you want your fixed-rate projects to be priced above how many hours at your hourly rate it would take. For example, you may charge $15,000 for a rewrite job that only takes you 20 hours.

Try to break down your freelancing income goals into weekly chunks to make them more manageable. Some months, you may exceed your goals. That's great! Just don't spend it all in one place. Freelancing can be feast-or-famine, so make sure you're reserving savings for months with less income. *Cough* Like summer months. *Cough*

Eventually, you should also think about building out passive income streams like dividend stocks, e-books, courses, affiliate marketing, and other forms of income. This will help take the burden off of your "active" income like freelancing. (More on that later in this book!)

While you may not start at your target hourly rate, know that you'll get there over time. That's why if you have a day job, it's smart to not quit right away, or to only quit when you have savings in the bank to cushion any rocky starts.

...But What About Taxes?

I recommend talking with a CPA on your self-employed tax rate and what that could look like. It can get complicated: especially if you have an entity (such as an LLC) that pays you through the company's payroll systems. I'm not a CPA, so I don't want to talk out of turn here (none of this is financial advice—just my experience!), but depending on your situation you can write off quite a bit on your taxes, such as any business expenses, business travel, and things like your home office.

For the sake of this exercise, I recommend adding a cushion to your expenses based on what your tax burden might be, and adjust it yearly as you get to know what your quarterly or annual taxes end up being with your unique situation.

Again, with my lawyer's eyes on me, none of this is financial advice, this is just my perspective on what's helped me. Cool? Cool.

In the next chapter, we'll take your new hourly rate and apply it to situations in which you should charge hourly versus fixed-rate for projects and clients!

Amy's Field Notes: If No One Tells You That You're Too Expensive, You're Not Charging Enough

"Only reply to this job post if you work at ten cents per word. I've met a lot of delusional writers lately," said a potential client's message to me on social media.

I replied and politely let him know his expectations were not in line with my rate (or the going rate for freelance writers of quality these days) and blocked him.

This isn't unusual: I've received many messages from disgruntled founders (usually those without funding or experience or any kind of success) who think my rate is too high. And yes, $350/hour is too high if you're not a legitimate business or if you don't put a high priority on written content. A $100/hour freelancer can do amazing work for the right business, but I'm not that writer. I used to be, but the demand for my time grew so large that I was forced to raise my rates to keep up with the number of incoming projects. That's just how the path from beginner to expert works.

A simple way to think about your hourly pricing? Start low, and increase your rates by $5/hour with every successful client and job. Increase by $10/hour every time you are so swamped with work that you can't handle your workload. Eventually, you'll hit your target hourly rate—and maybe even surpass it. A good test to see how you're doing? If no one is pushing back on your pricing, you're not charging enough.

If raising your rates feels awkward, you're not alone. We've been brainwashed into thinking our time isn't worth much. As an employee, you might have bought into the "scarcity mindset" that you would never be able to earn the money that was truly worth the value of your skills.

You'll also face bullies out there in the world when you raise your rates. There's nothing wrong with starting out at $30/hour and increasing your rate with experience as you learn—that's what I did. But there is something wrong with a potential client trying to make you feel bad for what your rates are currently.

When I run into someone who is trying to make me feel bad about what I charge, I realize the trolls are just jealous that I make more than them. I take a breath, log off, and look outside my window at the amazing view of the ocean I woke up to that morning, or stroll down a quaint street in Paris where I'm staying for the month.

Living well is the best revenge.

PART I: GETTING STARTED AS A FREELANCE WRITER

CHAPTER 5:
HOW TO PRICE YOUR PROJECTS AND GET PAID MORE

When understanding what to charge your clients for different projects, let's start with the difference between **fixed-rate** (aka flat fee) and **hourly** projects.

For an example, let's say I'm hiring you to write my memoir. I'm a hacker-turned-FBI-informant here to share with you why your computer can be the victim of my signature crime: forcing you to use the Microsoft software suite *forever*.

Anyways, when I come to you with my story, I ask: "how much will it cost?"

And to answer that, you as the freelance writer need to decide: am I going to charge hourly or a fixed-rate fee for this?

When to Charge a Fixed-Rate Fee

Whenever you're thinking about pricing, you need to balance your needs as a freelance writer (paying the bills, working on projects that respect your time and experience) with your client's needs (receiving something of value, seeing a return on their investment.) Some freelancers only pick one payment structure (i.e., I go through periods of time where I only do hourly work) and other freelancers apply different payment structures to different types of clients.

Fixed-rate pricing is very popular for clients who want to know exactly the cost of a project upfront. You should charge a fixed-rate fee for projects with **super-clear** deliverables and guidelines.

For example, if your client knows they want you to write a 1,000-word article based on a talk the founder gave about how walkable cities cure cancer (I would believe it), that's a great deliverable to do a fixed-rate project for. You can quote them a flat fee—derived from your hourly rate!—and include up to two rewrites (or whatever other stipulations you decide.)

That work is clear, enforceable with a contract, and you can also estimate how long that project will take to complete even in the worst-case scenario.

To calculate your fixed rate, I recommend taking your hourly rate, multiplying it times the number of hours you think it will take you, and then add a 30% extra cushion onto the final rate to cover revisions and any unexpected twists or turns in the project.

I also recommend you get an **upfront deposit** before you begin work on a fixed-rate project. This is a non-refundable milestone for the first chunk of work you're embarking on, and it should be large enough to cover part of your time spent on the project if your client dips out and doesn't pay you for the second half.

I usually do a 50% upfront deposit unless the project is over $15,000. In that case, I break it up into milestones: 1/3 upfront, 1/3 upon deliverable of the rough draft(s), and 1/3 upon final revisions.

If a project goes beyond the scope of work (meaning, if the client wants you to do a bajillion more rewrites or add another deliverable to the job), make sure there is wording in your contract that explains you will charge any additional work at your hourly rate after notifying your client that the work they are requesting is beyond your fixed-rate agreement.

If you're freelancing on a freelance platform, you're probably working with the existing contract that platform provides, so just make sure you're getting the above in writing when you begin the contract with your client.

Otherwise, I highly recommend hiring a lawyer to create a contract template you can use and modify for every new client you take on. Trust me: it's worth the money as soon as you start freelancing off of freelance platforms.

✱ Quick Template: How to Share Your Project Quote Over Email

Just hopped off the phone with a client and need to email them a project quote? Here's a template for you:

Hello [Client],

It was great meeting you today and hearing about [Client's Company and/or Project]!

Here's my proposal for us to start working together:

Project Name: [NAME]
Deliverables: [DELIVERABLES]
Quote: [NUMBER]
Next steps: I bill [BILLING SCHEDULE]. To begin, I'll [NEXT STEPS, UPFRONT DEPOSIT, CONTRACT, ETC.].

Thanks, let me know if you'd like to move forward!

Best,

-Your Name

When to Charge Hourly

Charge an hourly rate when you're not entirely sure how long a project will take, or if there's a lot of back-and-forth revisions and complex aspects to the project.

For example, let's say I'm a founder of a grocery delivery company called *Traitor Jen* that doesn't betray their customers by paying drivers living wages and offering shoppers local options to purchase their groceries and trinkets. I want you to help with every aspect of our copy, from the landing page to the email drip campaign. I even want you to write an animated video series showcasing our hero, Traitor Jen herself, saving the world from wilted kale and the exploitative side effects of capitalism (both equally as bad!)

Because I want you to be in meetings and do a lot of work and scattered revisions, you would have a hard time constantly adjusting your quote and project fees. Instead, charge an hourly rate for projects like this. You can even set an hourly cap (i.e., 20 hours per week) so I know what to expect in terms of billing cycles with you while you're helping me save the world, one bag of groceries at a time.

Billing hourly is a great option if you have clients who want to work at their own pace with you and need a flexible option when it comes to their project. This is also great for clients who aren't quite sure what they need. Hourly billing can help focus a client to be as mindful of your time as possible: after all, it's costing them when they aren't. Working on an hourly basis protects you from scope creep and disorganization on the client's side of things.

When to Create a Monthly Retainer

If you're doing a long-term project, consider negotiating a monthly retainer.

Put simply, a monthly retainer is when your client "reserves" a certain number of hours per month of your time by paying upfront for that time.

Some retainers are negotiated so that your hours are use-it-or-lose-it. Any unused hours of your time don't roll over to the next month, and you have to be paid for those hours regardless of whether or not your client needs them. This is what I would recommend, because if you're not using a retainer this way, you're just working hourly.

Monthly retainers are great because you can know ahead of time how many hours you need to set aside for a project, and you can more accurately estimate how much you're going to make in a month. A taste of stability in an unstable world.

You should also stipulate that your client has to give you a 30-day notice if they decide to terminate your retainer. That way, you can plan if you need to increase your client outreach if your retainer client decides to bow out.

Personally, I prefer package and fixed-rate pricing these days (more on packages later!) but sometimes opt for hourly-only projects depending on my schedule. I've worked on a retainer once before, and it was nice when I was getting started, but now I prefer the flexibility of canceling hourly contracts if I want to shift to new projects rather than having to wait a whole month to get out of a retainer.

At the end of the day, it's all about what you want to optimize for. Freedom? Recurring income and long-term clients? Or new and exciting projects that allow you the ability to work with a variety of clients?

Experiment to see what works for you: you might find that your preferences change depending on what your needs are.

Later in the book, I'll dive into package pricing and other clever, value-based pricing models you can use to land jobs and leverage your talents while giving clients an awesome experience.

How to Double Your Income When Demand Outweighs Supply

I started my freelancing career at around $35/hour and kept increasing my rates with each job from there until I got to my rate of $350/hour as of the writing of this book.

A good rule is that whenever you have more projects than you know what to do with, the universe is telling you to double your rates. Rinse and repeat with every instance you feel overloaded.

Unsure if that strategy is going to work? Let's do some math:

Let's say I'm a new freelancer and I'm charging $50/hour and have five clients who fill up about thirty billable hours per week. That means I'm making **$1,500 every week** with my current client load.

Now, let's say I have five more clients who want to hire me. I know I won't be able to handle all ten of these clients at the moment, but I'd also like to level up. Because I'm at the point where client demand is higher than the supply of my time, I can decide to **double my hourly rate**.

If I double my hourly rate for both my current and new clients, then I may lose two current clients and three potential clients, which leaves me with five current clients. That's the same number I had before—but now

I'm charging $100/hour. So, I'm now making **$3,000 every week** and I'm working the same number of billable hours.

And *that's* how you scale your freelance business—without becoming an agency or overloading your workload.

As you get better at doing your job and expand the ways potential new clients can find you, you'll continuously get overwhelmed with too much incoming work, which means you can keep raising your rates.

No Unpaid Test Assignments

"Would you mind doing this super quick test task? It'll help us get to know you."

I was working from the dining table of our Airbnb in Venice, Italy, and my freelance business was doing really well. But when this message came in from a potential client, I felt torn. The people-pleasing side of me wanted to complete the unpaid test task they had requested.

So, I did. And then the client ghosted. No feedback, no response… until I saw another job post a few days later, the client once again requesting writers to complete a "super short" unpaid test task.

That's when I realized: *he was putting together his copy based on free work from a bunch of writers on this platform.* What an exploitative way to get your web copy written.

From that point on, I've never done free work for anyone, ever again. I never begin work until I have a contract and a 50% upfront deposit in place, either.

Raising Your Rates Solves All Your Problems

I want to hammer this point home: *raising your rates as a freelancer solves all your problems.*

Too many clients? Raise your rates and now you'll only have clients that can pay your new rate. Feeling overwhelmed by fast deadlines? Raise your rates by charging a rush fee so you can clear your schedule. Feeling like your clients aren't appreciative of your work? Raise your rates so only people who see and value your skill work with you.

The only thing that isn't solved by raising your rates is if you have *too few* incoming clients. To solve that, you need more experience, a better portfolio, social proof, and more ways for you to find clients—and for them to find you.

Don't worry: the rest of the book covers all of that, and I'll help you hit the joyful part of your career when you become an in-demand freelance writer so you can work on your terms.

Amy's Field Notes: People Value What They Pay For

I used to host open mic nights at a studio space in Los Angeles. My co-founder and I would invite musicians, dancers, and storytellers to come and share their art under one roof, and we handled all of the marketing of the event, too.

At first, we contemplated just selling tickets at the door. They were only $5 after all: why not just have people show up?

But I decided to have an online ticket sales section of our website where people could pay ahead of time. That way, we could get a sense of how many people were going to show up.

As it turned out, selling tickets ahead of time helped us to sell way more tickets. We sold out our first few shows, and the one show we didn't push the buying-tickets-ahead-of-time angle, we had a half-empty audience.

The lesson? Even if it's $5, people fall into the "sunken cost fallacy" where they're more likely to show up if they've spent money already on something. Get people to invest in your event, your services as a freelancer, and they're more likely to show up and appreciate your hard work.

Offer something for free—or don't get them to pay upfront—and they might not value it as much.

PART I: GETTING STARTED AS A FREELANCE WRITER

CHAPTER 6:
HOW TO BUILD YOUR FREELANCE WRITING PORTFOLIO

When it comes to being a successful freelancer, you need to begin by building a cool-as-hell portfolio that shows your range and depth of skills.

Your portfolio can contain stuff you've written for clients, a poem you wrote to a long-lost lover, some thoughts you scribbled on the back of your family's banana bread recipe while you were contemplating life as the bread rose in the oven—whatever. Your portfolio should contain written work that shows people who you are and what you're capable of.

But, in an ideal world, your portfolio also contains something similar to what your ideal clients want to hire you to write—not just that novel that's part one of a ten-part series that you've been working on for ten years. (Don't @ me, we all have one of those!)

Practice in Public

I get a lot of questions from new freelancers asking how to build their portfolio if they don't have any clients or experience. To be honest, most of the clients I've worked with hired me off of my blog over at AmySuto.com. That's crazy considering I mostly write about that one time I failed a pasta making class in Italy. (Almost as embarrassing as the time I almost failed my pass/fail Geology class at USC because I was sleeping with my study partner. There's a joke about rocks in here but I'm not going to make it.)

Anyways, when I talk about "practicing in public" I mean that no matter what type of freelancer you are, you should be sharing your skills and sharpening them on a public forum. I practice my famed witticisms on my blog, newsletter, and social media, and recommend you do the same.

As a writer, you probably have ambitions of writing the next Great American Novel while also being a freelancer as your "day job" of sorts. That's actually great, because you can show off your chops by publishing short stories. One of my short stories about how depressing being a Hollywood assistant was landed me a bunch of my favorite clients. They didn't just pity the past version of myself: they appreciated my pithy prose that only the dregs of Hollywood could summon.

Another way to get your work out there is to submit your personal essays to publications. That's what I did when I came out as bisexual through a personal essay in the Los Angeles Times. Just live your life online, y'all. It's as easy-peasy and very-scary as that. As long as you're staying true to yourself and sharing things you're comfortable with, you'll strike a chord with readers.

Be sure to stay in your authentic voice, though. Trying to be someone else takes *way* too much time and energy, and it'll show in your work if you're not being real. All plants grow towards the sun. We as humans all have our own internal suns, so grow towards that source of light and you'll save yourself a lot of heartache.

Practicing in public is how you get better and also show off what you're learning to people who are looking to hire you. So, start that blog and get scribbling.

Prompts for "Fictional" Portfolio Pieces

When I'm working with my one-on-one coaching clients[3], I like to provide "prompts" to help the writers I mentor build out their portfolio so they can land clients. For example, if you're a copywriter in the skincare space but don't have enough portfolio items to land jobs, I create little prompts using fake skincare brands that you will write for.

While you need to be honest with potential clients that these portfolio items are not for real companies, they still are a great sample of your

---

3   Want to see if I'm currently accepting new coaching clients? Visit: amysuto.com/six-figure-freelancer

work across different mediums and can lead to more jobs.

You can do this exercise yourself! I'll put some general prompts below to help spark portfolio piece ideas:

- **Email Copywriting Prompt:** Find a brand or company in your niche that you love. Imagine they are having a seasonal sale or exclusive discount on their product or services, and write a one-hundred-word email that would go to their subscribers. Be sure to write the subject line, email summary line (the one that shows up in people's inboxes before they click on it!), and the body text. Bonus points if you can recommend how a designer would design the graphic elements of the email :)

- **Web Copywriting Prompt:** Hunt down a landing page or homepage of a website you think has epic copy—preferably for a company you've recently bought from, which shows that their copy was good enough to persuade you to buy! Then, create a "mirror universe" version of their brand (such as my fictional Traitor Jen's grocery delivery company for good) and write a landing page using your own copy to sell consumers on why it's so great. Be persuasive and concise: keep your copy under 500 words!

- **Longform Blog Post or Article Prompt:** This prompt is for all you content writers out there. Write a blog post or article about a topic in your niche. Make sure the topic is evergreen: something that won't age too poorly in your portfolio. I recommend writing a staple piece explaining something super foundational in your niche (such as "color theory 101" or "what is the blockchain") and explain it with a clever, witty voice and make sure you include citations and statistics that you've researched. A good length for a sample article can be anywhere from 800-1,000 words.

You can use these prompts (or any ideas of your own!) to generate as many portfolio pieces as you need to round out your portfolio.

Building Your Portfolio and Social Proof

When you're landing those early clients, it's imperative that you're asking them if it's okay to use the work you're doing in your portfolio. If they say no, all good. Not every client will be cool with you adding the work you do for them to your public portfolio, so just know it may take some time for you to build up to the point where you have a decent amount of material and social proof of your services.

Also ask if they can leave you a review if you're freelancing on a platform, or to send you a testimonial if you're freelancing in the wild. If they're not comfortable with leaving you a public review, an anonymous testimonial will do as well.

I recommend building a "post-job" workflow where you ask every client for a review, whether or not you can use the material in your portfolio, and to even maybe give them a discount on their next project with you. Even better if you can use tools to automate this workflow with a post-project questionnaire—but more on that later.

✳ Quick Template: Asking for a Testimonial

Here's a common template I use when I'm asking a client to write (or film!) a written or video testimonial for me.

Hi [Client Name],
It was great working on [name of your last project] with you. I'm so impressed by what you're building at [company name] and would love to offer you a 10% discount on any next project you do with me.

Oh, and if you enjoyed working with me, would you mind leaving me a review? [Insert link] It helps me continue to work with awesome people like yourself.

Thanks!
-[Your Name]

Do a Portfolio Audit Every Six Months

As a freelance writer, I recommend you revisit your portfolio, website, and profile every six months and do an audit.

Ask yourself the following questions:

- Am I attracting my ideal clients?
- Is there a freelance writing niche I want to move into but don't have samples for?
- What portfolio items should I generate next to get the type of clients I want?
- Are there samples that no longer represent who I am as a writer that I need to replace?
- Does my portfolio show my personality as a writer and a freelancer?

The goal here is to never say "I don't have that" when a client asks you for a sample of a type of work you like to do. The last thing you want is to spend your life pining for the opportunity to write a commercial jingle, and then not have a sample of your jingle-writing abilities when a brand comes to you asking for a sample!

The lesson? Always be building your portfolio!

Build Your Freelancing Portfolio While Beating Imposter Syndrome

The only thing stronger than my imposter syndrome is my desire to Make Cool Things. If you're someone who (also) struggles with showcasing their skills, I've got news for you.

There's someone out there that's half as talented as you charging three times what you're charging. There's a shortage of skilled freelancers, and the world needs you. Seriously. People talk all the time about the freelance platforms being oversaturated. That's not true (trust me—I hire freelancers all the time for my own work!).

So, don't worry too much about whether or not something is good or not. Just post it. Keep refining your skills, but know that your skills get better by accumulating your 10,000 hours. You can always go back and edit your portfolio or your blog later (do you know how many posts I've deleted that were written by my 12-year-old self? So many.)

Have the confidence to back up your work, even if you're faking it until you make it. Just remember: we're all living in a simulation, so just play the game and have some fun while doing it.

Amy's Field Notes: Freelancing is a Garden That Grows Over Time

I got very into gardening before I was a digital nomad. By "very into gardening" I, of course, mean the radishes I was growing had been close to death several times before I eventually drowned them with water. However, I did have some produce to show for my efforts, and made some tiny garden salads fit for ants.

Gardening fascinates me because I can walk out into a garden and see totally new growth of my plants that feels surprising and satisfying. I can also walk outside after neglecting them for a week and see that yes, plants do need water and some TLC to survive (who knew?)

I see freelancing much like building a garden. It takes time (and consistent watering!) to grow. Sometimes you'll kill a plant, or sometimes you'll realize you need a different type of soil or different amount of sunlight for it to thrive. You need both gardening knowledge as well as a stomach for trial-and-error to get a good green thumb.

I've been freelancing for about seven years as of the writing of this book, but I really kickstarted my full-time freelance writing career in summer of 2020. Before then, I didn't take it seriously: it was a part-time thing I did in-between jobs.

But when I really committed to watering my own garden? It grew on a daily basis, and I'm able to enjoy a hard-won bounty.

There's something so satisfying about growing what you eat and being able to provide for yourself, so take the time to sow the seeds of your portfolio so you can harvest the results later at an epic dinner party.

PART I: GETTING STARTED AS A FREELANCE WRITER

CHAPTER 7:
FREELANCE PLATFORMS AND FINDING GREAT CLIENTS

When I first started as a new freelancer, I began on the platform Upwork. That platform helped me get to where I am today: as of the writing of this book (at the end of 2022), I've earned over $280,000 on Upwork, and much more off of the platform. I can buy quite a few slices of avocado toast with that money (*shhh* don't tell the Boomers!)

If you're a new freelancer, I recommend getting started on a freelance platform. These platforms provide infrastructure to help you get the hang of freelancing while you're still building up your career. These platforms are also helpful for anyone currently freelancing in the "side hustle" space who doesn't have the time or means to get all of their own freelance systems up and running yet.

In this chapter, I'll dive into the pros and cons of freelance platforms as a whole, and how to navigate them. Because freelance platforms change aspects of their features every year or so, I also have courses available on my website that break down the nuances of these platforms and are updated alongside any new features that come out.[4]

---

4   For more online resources, you can go to: amysuto.com/six-figure-freelancer for my most up-to-date guides, courses, and freelancing platform recommendations.

Pros and Cons of Freelancing Platforms

Freelance platforms are great because they provide structure to the freelancing process, and also help you get connected to clients. They're a great marketing tool, as you can showcase public reviews and build trust with potential clients.

The downside of these platforms is that they often take a large chunk of your earnings and can charge you additional fees for submitting proposals or using their platform.

Another downside is that you can't customize the contracts on these platforms, which can lead to being unable to hold your client responsible if they don't pay you, and some other sticky legal situations. You're better protected if you're working off of your own contract that you develop with a trusted lawyer.

So be aware of what the terms and conditions are with any freelance platform you're interacting with, and do your best to play by the rules.

Finding Great Clients in the World Wide Web and Beyond

You shouldn't rely on freelancing platforms forever: these platforms can unexpectedly ban you, shut down, or not have the clients that are best suited to you.

That's why you should be doing as many of the below as you can:

- **Create your own blog and website.** Write articles that feature keywords your ideal clients within your niche are searching. My blog at AmySuto.com has gone after keywords like "memoir ghostwriter," landing me on the front page of Google, and has brought me hundreds of thousands of dollars in freelance business.

- **Optimize your social media.** Make sure all of your social media has links to your freelance website or blog, and people know you're available to be hired for freelance work. If you don't want to use your personal accounts, create new accounts just for your freelance work. Make sure you're using searchable keywords in all of your profiles and name fields.

PART I: GETTING STARTED AS A FREELANCE WRITER

- **Go to conferences, events, and other places your ideal clients hang out at.** This could be something as simple as joining a co-working space, or as complex as tracking down conferences and other industry events around the world specific to your niche.

- **Create a newsletter and send out updates weekly.** Put the sign-up form on your website, get your clients to subscribe, and keep them in the loop with what you're doing. That way, you'll be top-of-mind when it's time for them to hire for a new writing project.

- **When in doubt, return to the art of the freelance platform proposal and cold email.** We'll talk about this in a moment, but the most important thing you can do every day is to reach out to potential clients who need your services. If you're a freelancer, this last bullet point will be the most important part of your day-to-day tasks until you start landing clients!

Your goal as a freelancer is to become a magnet for all you want to attract. And until you've graduated from fridge magnet to an epic superconductor magnet, you'll need to put in the daily work to bring your ideal clients to you.

✷ Quick Tip: Your Personal Brand vs. Your Freelancing Brand

If you're a creative professional like I am, you may want to know if it's best to split your "personal/creative" brand from your "freelancing" brand. You may think that things will be cleaner if you have a separate set of social media accounts and a separate freelancing website *just* for your freelance business. Be wary of this impulse. I thought that was the right move, too, but as of the end of 2022 I'm actually consolidating my freelance website into my personal "AmySuto.com" blog. Instead of having two websites, I'm just creating a separate page for my freelance work so that I can take advantage of that web traffic and not have to maintain two separate sites. Chances are, your freelance clients are more likely to find you through your creative work or personal accounts/blog, so why not just put everything in one place? It will also help you stay more consistent with your content creation if everything has a home under your name. Instead of getting super niche and separating out your identities, I think the future will belong to those who make their unique collection of interests and identities a niche in itself! You can be both a fantasy novelist and a travel writer: you'd be surprised how your audiences might overlap in surprising ways!

Crafting the Perfect Cover Letter and Proposal Letter

Part of finding great clients is sending out (daily!) proposals on freelancing platforms and cold-emailing clients you find out in the world. You need to keep doing this until your roster is full, so make outreach part of your daily habits.

Not sure what to put in your cover letter/proposal? No big deal! Use the below template to get started. I've geared this one specifically for freelance platforms, but you can remove that language and easily use this for non-freelance-platform, cold reach-outs as well.

As a reminder, make sure to personalize most if not all of the cover letters you send out. This will help increase your hits and likelihood of being awarded a contract.

The Template

Hi! My name is **{NAME}** and I am a **{creative copywriter/memoir ghostwriter/INSERT NICHE HERE}** based in **{CITY}**. I'm also a **{RISING TALENT/TOP RATED/TOP RATED PLUS}** freelancer here on **{FREELANCE PLATFORM}**, which means I'm in the top **{n/a/10%/3%}** of talent here on **{FREELANCE PLATFORM}**!

My work has been featured in… **{put any press here!}**

My rate is **{hourly rate}** but I'd be happy to chat about fixed-rate projects as well. **{You can also put a link to any package rates here as well!}**

{ADD MORE PERSONALIZATION HERE: what else can you say about why you're a great fit for this specific job?}

Here's my calendar link if you'd like to hop on a free 30-minute discovery call! **{insert calendar link}**

More about me: **{include more biographical details, a link to your website and/or portfolio, your best work, etc.}**
I also… **{include more services you offer outside of your niche, or in addition to your main workload. i.e., if you offer consulting or writing coaching or editing on top of ghostwriting.}**

Here's what my clients say about me:

{INSERT TESTIMONIALS}

I love doing great work for my clients, and I'd love to help you with this project!

Looking forward to hearing from you,

-{YOUR NAME}

It's as simple as that! Now get out there and start sharing your services with the world.

Get Your Clients on a Call, Fast!

I'll talk a bit more about the tools I use in my client pipeline later in the automations chapter, but I wanted to bring up a critical piece of landing great clients.

Make their experience as frictionless as possible.

For example, if you're a new freelancer, don't just send clients a proposal on a freelancing platform asking them to let you know if they want to hop on a call with you. Send them your calendar link and invite them to book a free discovery call with you—right in your proposal/sales letter.

Same thing with your website: don't make them dig through your pages to find your contact form. Put the contact form on your homepage, and list options of your packages for them to purchase to get them thinking about how they want to work with you.

Keep optimizing for a smoother, steadier client pipeline. Try and get them on a call with you in as few steps as possible!

Then, when you're overwhelmed with leads, you can remove your link from the cover letter and add some extra steps to screen clients before they get on a call with you. Get the ball rolling first, and then take steps to be picky when you're magnetized as hell and attracting all of the amazing people you want to work with.

Amy's Field Notes: Crossing the Threshold

My partner Kyle has a great term for doing things we're uncomfortable with: *crossing the threshold*. I've also heard that the happiness of a life can be measured in how many hard conversations we were able to have, or even that "you miss all the shots you don't take."

Some of the best moments in my life arose from shooting a shot. Whether it was going up to someone at a bar and saying hello, or telling a friend I had romantic feelings for them, or asking someone to vouch for me in my career—the good things came from those scary moments of crossing a threshold.

Sometimes, crossing a threshold might be swallowing your nerves on a client call and explaining with confidence why you're the perfect writer for the job. Or, it might be sending a cold email to a company you want to work with, and pitching yourself and your services.

One of my favorite jobs I've landed came from crossing several thresholds: first, I cold-emailed the company because I saw what they were building and thought it was amazing. I wanted to work with them, but after a few meetings, I saw them trying to put me in a role that wasn't quite a fit for my skills, so I told them (honestly) what would and wouldn't work for me. That honest conversation could have ruled me out as a candidate, but it helped me land the job. In the same role, I've had to carve out my responsibilities within the company, pitching ideas and setting boundaries within the team.

The confidence I have now has come from a deep, consistent crossing of thresholds. I didn't start out this way: I had to push through discomfort to get to a better, happier new world.

So, if you feel uncomfortable or nervous, know that's just part of life. Cross the threshold anyways, sweaty palms and all: you never know what's waiting for you on the other side.

PART I: GETTING STARTED AS A FREELANCE WRITER

CHAPTER 8:
TAKING THE CALL: LANDING A CLIENT

You did it! You impressed with a headshot of you doing tricks at the skate park or something, your bio brags about how many hot chili peppers you can eat in under forty-five seconds, and you're ready to work with some clients!

But wait. You have to actually sell yourself to a potential client on the discovery call they booked with you. How exactly does one do that?

Fake It 'Till You Make It

The first freelance assignment I ever had was when I was sixteen. I lied, said I was eighteen, and got them to send me cash to shoot and edit some short "how-to" videos that still exist on their website to this day. I made good money, about $300 a video, and my clients were none the wiser that a minor was shooting and editing their content from her parent's backyard.

While I recommend that you don't outright *lie* to your clients, you should still embody the energy of a sixteen-year-old who thinks they're invincible. If that's not the energy that resonates with you, that's cool, just tap into whatever confidence source moves you. Whether that's professional, calm and collected, or energetic and passionate—do that!

I've won out on huge jobs against *very established writers* with published books and who had decades of experience on me.

Why? I literally asked one of my clients that.

"Because you had more passion," my client told me.

Even though I was twenty-six at the time, I was being entrusted with huge books. Books that were about murders, cold-cases, redemption—I was being entrusted with people's life stories and being paid tens of thousands of dollars to do so.

My resume didn't matter: what mattered was that I had a passion for my work and care for my clients. And that care showed up on the page and in my meetings with clients.

So, when you're talking to clients, it doesn't matter that you don't have a million years of experience or published books to your name. What matters is that you confidently share what you bring to the table—which is a lot! And if you're feeling down on yourself, return to your "why" and then fake it 'till you make it.

If you lack experience, you can make it up in passion and perspective. Own that. Don't ever let someone try and undervalue you because you're not some Nobel Laureate. Most published authors write boring books that suck. Some are great, but most aren't. I guarantee you can do better than a stuffy professor who has to write a book to keep their tenure.

At the end of the day, I guarantee you that if you are reading these words, you're a damn good writer. Why? Because you care about learning and have great taste already because you're reading this book. So many people call themselves writers but never put in the work. Their work suffers, and they don't have the pride in the process or customer service that you need to be a successful freelancer.

So, wear your confidence proudly. Even if you feel anxious or underprepared, step up to the plate and give it your best shot. If they don't work with you, that's their loss. Every "no" pushes you closer to your "yes," where you're truly meant to be. Every potential client call gives you a chance to practice and get closer, so enjoy the chance up at bat.

How to Prepare for a Call

If a client has sent you over any files or links to check out before your call, make sure to read them thoroughly and be able to reference anything in them.

Also, do your research: Google a client and get a sense of who they are and what they've been up to. Don't be creepy by bringing up too much about them on the call—let them tell you about them. But doing this client research can help you figure out what kind of questions to ask.

If they haven't sent you their company website, see if it's in their email address if that's available to you. Do your best to get as much context as possible going into the call, and see if there's a touchstone or something you have in common with your client.

When you're creating availability on your calendar tool or other scheduling system for discovery calls, don't forget to give yourself breaks in-between calls. Everyone knows I'm a masochist when it comes to batching all my discovery calls on one day (let's do thirteen calls back-to-back no breaks, baby!!!) but in recent times, I've made an effort to be more mindful with my schedule (can you tell my villain era is behind me?) I recommend scheduling in breaks between every call or two so that you have some time to decompress, check emails, take notes, and add anything to your task list that pertains to the call you just had.

On the Discovery Call

Ready to discover some great clients? No snakes here, Indiana Jones, just some of my top tips for impressing on a potential client call:

- **Practice your brief one- to two-minute "headline" about who you are, what you do, and what your superpowers are.** I always bring up my TV and film experience because my clients like to know about my background of working in Hollywood and being trained in storytelling. I also talk about growing up in a small town in Arizona where people ride horses to work, and often run into fellow equestrian aficionados. Give people touchstones about you that they can relate to mixed in with impressive professional accomplishments or details about your strengths and skills.

- **Spend most of the call listening and asking questions.** I spend 80% of my calls with potential clients and clients listening. I spend the other 20% simply sharing my experience and advice and asking and answering questions. Be prepared with questions you can ask to show that you read anything they sent along and are interested in. Understand what they're looking for from a writer.

Not sure what to ask? **I love asking the following questions:**

- Why do you want to tell this story/why did you start this company/why do you care about this industry?
- Tell me more about you and your company.
- What are you looking for in a writer?
- What's your timeline for this project?
- Do you have a budget for this project?
- What are your goals for this project? (Do you want to get this book published the traditional route or do you want to self-publish and just distribute to your family? Etc.)

Gather information, and send the quote and proposal later. I usually approach these calls pretty informally. I love to chat up a potential client, feel them out, get to know them and what they're looking for, and then tell them I'm going to follow-up with a quote and a proposal/plan of action. (More on that in a sec!)

Generally, it's best to separate the "money stuff" from the "fun stuff." Money is often a pain point for people, so the more you can separate the finance stuff from your personal interactions with them, the better. However, some clients will ask for a quote or your broad price range on a call. Have some numbers prepared before the call, but still be very firm and say you'll follow up with a quote.

If a client asks you for a quote on the call, you can simply just say something like:

- I'll send over my price list after we hop off.
- Great question, let me create a custom quote for you and I'll email it to you after our call today.
- Let me go through your materials and I'll get back to you over email before end of day with my quote.

In addition, you'll probably want to take a look at any materials they currently have—such as a partial draft or company branding materials—before formulating a quote, as you don't want to be surprised by something they failed to mention on the call that might impact scope of work.

✸ Quick Tip: Don't Be Shy About Money, Honey

While I think it's beneficial to make a connection with your client first before "talking money" as a new freelancer, eventually you'll get to the point where you'll need to screen clients before they hop on a call with you to see if they got the juice to hire you. This can be done by sharing with them a price list and asking if you fit in their budget, or sending a custom quote survey so they can peruse different pricing and discount options before meeting with you. Or, you can simply include in your cover letter that you have a policy where your project minimum is $5,000 over x period of time, and that can be organized as a project fee or bucket of hours. In short? Don't screen for budget when you're a beginner, but when you become more expensive, you'll have to be upfront about your dollar signs before you chat with companies and clients in order to protect your time.

Writing Up a Post-Call Follow-Up Email

Okay, so you had a fun time with your potential client, you guys bonded over your hopes/dreams/fears/hometowns/whatever and are swapping playlists and are friends on Facebook/LinkedIn/Myspace now. Great!

Now it's time to get down to business.

After you hop off your call, chat with your client about a quote if they asked you for one, and send over any additional info about how you two can work together. (If they're down to work with you, skip this step!)

Your potential client may respond to your post-call follow-up message in a number of ways:

1. *Potential Client:* You're cool and I love your music taste but God you're expensive, I can't afford you.

Which you can respond in one of two ways:

Response #1: You're cool too but I can't work below my rate, best of luck!
Response #2: I believe in this project so much I'll work below my rate just for you!

2. *Potential Client:* Can you send me more information/more samples/more references/more details about your process?

Your response: you can go ahead and send them more info: a lot of people like to do their due diligence.

3. *Potential Client:* Let's do the thing!!!

Your response: you pop champagne or a tasteful, artisan non-alcoholic ginger drink and celebrate!!!

From there, follow any next steps: lay down the timeline for the project, and as soon as they've signed the contract and paid your upfront deposit, it's time to begin!

The Art of Negotiation

If you find yourself struggling with the "negotiation" aspect of freelancing, this section is for you. I'll devote a separate chapter entirely to negotiating, but these are the headlines you need to know when you're just getting started.

Negotiating is a lot like dating. If you seem desperate or needy or too persistent, your potential client will be turned off by that. Instead, remember that there are a lot of fish in the sea, no client *is* the sea and *they* should be trying to convince *you* to work with them just as much as the other way around.

This mindset will help you negotiate like a pro!

Here are my top three tips for negotiating with clients to get paid more:

1. **Try and set yourself up for success before you even hop on a call with a client.** Make your hourly rate and package fees publicly available, and if you have a project minimum, make sure they know that as well before they even hop on a call with you.

2. **Collect social proof (i.e., client testimonials and case studies!) to increase trust with your potential client.** Keep building out your portfolio and create case studies on your website walking clients through past projects and how you were an integral part of their success. Find ways to be recognized in the press or be invited to speak at different events if you're really an overachiever (more on that later!)

3. **If your client asks if your rate is negotiable, say no.** I don't think freelancers' rates should be negotiated. I think the process of negotiation should mostly be you, the freelancer, assessing a client and their project, calculating a rate, and then sticking to that rate. If your client counters and comes back with a lower rate, you can decide if that's what you want to take. Generally, I find that any client trying to pull down your rate too heavily probably isn't going to be a great client to work with, especially if you were upfront on your rates in all of your materials and website. The only exception for this is that you can create package rates and discounts based on fixed-rate projects, but I consider this an advanced strategy so I'll go over that later in the book!

The reason why I like sending a quote in an email after a discovery call is because when the quote is written down it feels final, and usually that's the number that sticks. But if your potential client is asking for a number on a call with them, instead, give them a large range and say that you need to see the current draft or more details to come up with a full quote.

For example, when asked how much my rate is for developmental editing on a manuscript, on a phone call I'll say it depends on how much work needs to be done on the draft and how long it is, but my rate can range from ABC-XYZ. Generally, I end up charging around ABC, but I put a really high number on the high end so that it feels like they're getting a deal at where we land.

If a client is trying to negotiate you down, always try and counter with an in-between number that's halfway between yours and theirs. Or, if their number is ridiculously low, just say that you can't work below your rate—your number is final and that's how it is.

If you're sticking to your guns on your rate, you can rationally and calmly explain this is what you charge because you've got to justify the time spent on a project, because saying yes to this project means saying no to another.

But at the end of the day, you don't have to justify yourself. You charge what you charge, and I would recommend staying strong because often clients will come and meet you at your rate.

The Deal is Done!

You sent your proposal and quote, your client agreed, and BAM! The deal is done!

From there, do a great job for your client, rinse and repeat.

Amy's Field Notes: You Determine Your Value

A $100 bill is still a $100 bill, even if you crumple it up or fold it into an origami-style paper crane.

This also is true for your own skills. You are always inherently valuable: you just have to find the environment (and the clients!) that will see you and your skills for how valuable they are.

A perfect example of this is when I was doing my last job as a Hollywood assistant. I was working in a writers' room with a lovely group of people on a show I thought was full of heart and made with some true care. At the job, I wasn't making a whole lot—maybe $18 per hour or something similar—although the hours were easy and the job didn't take too much out of me.

In the mornings before I went into the writers' room, I would drive to a nearby coffee shop at 6am to beat traffic and do some freelance writing before I came in. The writing I did in those early mornings with a bagel and some hot coffee would net me $90 per hour. Then, after a few hours of banking some serious cash, I would walk into the writers' room and take notes for $18/hour—a $72/hour discount on my time.

At a certain point in that room, I realized I could never take a writers' assistant job again. It just wasn't making sense, and my skills weren't being valued in a way I saw them being valued outside of Hollywood.

Since that job, I've left Hollywood and have never looked back. Now, I make more than I ever could have in Hollywood, and I've been able to write and produce my own material—no network approval required!

This concept is the same when you consider how a baseball card might appear worthless if it's in a shoebox in your dad's closet, but on eBay it could fetch thousands of dollars. Or how an old car might look like a junker on a used car lot, but appraised by the right appreciator of antique cars, it could go for hundreds of thousands of dollars.

It's up to you to find the people and environments that value you for what your skills are actually worth. Don't settle for the lowest bidder.

PART 1: GETTING STARTED AS A FREELANCE WRITER

CHAPTER 9:
NO BLOG NO LIFE: BUILDING YOUR FREELANCING WEBSITE

Do you want tech companies to control your income forever? No? Then it's time to think about creating your own freelance services website and blog.

Do I sound dramatic? Not if you want to truly own your career without middlemen!

Freelance Platforms are Not Your Friend

During the writing of this book, I got a notification from a freelance platform I'm on:

> *Your account has been suspended. If you wish to appeal, please respond to this email.*

I checked my freelance account, and sure enough, I couldn't log in. I couldn't access any messages, projects, money, or proposals. They were all… **poof** gone.

If I had received this message earlier in my career when I depended on these platforms to get leads, then this could have been a huge blow. At certain points in time, I've had up to tens of thousands of dollars sitting in escrow on freelance platforms: losing that would have been an enormous hit.

This story has a happy ending: first, at this point in time I don't rely on freelance platforms for most of my business. They maybe bring in about 10-20% of my leads. And second, when I emailed the platform to appeal, they gave me the account back hours later.

However, they did not reinstate the money I had spent on proposals, and I took a small hit to the tune of a few hundred dollars.

In summary? The work done on freelancing platforms is not your own. You have to own your own leads if you want to own your own business.

Be Like the Mafia: Why You Should Own Your Own Block

Okay, maybe don't be *exactly* like the mafia. We don't need more broken legs or bad attempts at Italian accents out there. But you shouldn't build on rented land: you need to own your own website domain and build your leads organically through search.

Now some of you may argue that using a third-party website builder is *still* bowing to another huge tech platform. And yeah, sure. If you want to be totally decentralized, there are other options. But a website builder isn't going to police your leads and communication with clients, so there's that.

How I Earn $100,000+ from My Website Every Year

One of my most recent clients found me through a search engine. He stumbled upon a blog article I had written about memoirs, and emailed me asking if he could hire me. I agreed, and I landed over $100,000 worth of business from that one client.

Countless other leads have come in from my blog articles: people find me, they approve of my weird dad jokes, and are like "hey, kid, why don't you come bring some of that spice over here?" and then we get cookin'.

I also leverage my website and newsletter for brand deals and affiliate links, which nets me thousands of dollars each month. Not bad for just spilling the tea in some blog posts if you ask me.

What I'm trying to say here is that your website is an investment. You have to invest first your time and then sometimes money to build, design, and update your site.

Elements of a Great Freelancing Website

Every freelancer's website will be a little different: your personality, services, and ideal clients are unique to you, after all.

But when it comes to the basics, here are all the elements you'll need to convince some strangers to spend some cash on you:

- **Tell people what you do on your homepage.** When someone lands on the homepage of your website, it should be super easy for them to click buttons to hire you, read your blog, or check out your portfolio—without having to scroll too far down. People are lazy and have short attention spans: make the actions you want them to take easy and obvious!

- **Get personal.** Include your headshot, bio, and an "about me" page or section. People work with people, not robots, so put yourself out there. Keep your clients' needs front-and-center (they're here to solve their problem, after all) but make sure they still feel like they're getting to know you without having to read your life story on your homepage.

- **Host your portfolio on your website.** Your portfolio should be beautiful and accessible. You could just link to a portfolio PDF for clients to download, but I recommend having some links on your website so those who are averse to downloading things can check out some of your stuff right on your site.

- **Have a clear "work with me" landing page with your services.** This could be your homepage or a separate page. Either way, lay out your services and the value you provide to clients and create a clear call-to-action (CTA) where clients can either fill out a contact form or book a free discovery call with you. (Pick one or the other!)

- **If you're an expert, include case studies.** Did you land a past client a ton of new clicks or sales? People LOVE to see that you can get them results, so if you have shareable graphs, charts, or other metrics that shows the value of your work, include this on your landing page and also have breakout case studies.

- **Include testimonials.** Share the love from past clients. Include any social proof you have access to: testimonials, awards you've won, and any press you may have gotten. This will help build trust with you and your ideal clients.

Your website should be authentic to you, your services, and what you provide to clients. When in doubt, ask for feedback from your clients or friends and family on how your website looks and feels.

How to Land Clients Organically, Without Having to Find Them

When I say organic, I'm not talking about expensive produce: organic traffic to your website is the free stuff, the kind that search engines fork over to you when you've got the good stuff on your blog. Your goal as a freelancer is to build a blog that ranks for the keywords your ideal clients are searching for.

Keywords, simply put, are what your ideal clients are typeity-type-typing into their search engine to find an answer for something. You want your content to be the answer to that question (if it's a question related to your business, of course.)

Here are the **three ways** to get organic traffic from your website:

- **Post two blog posts a week.** Write two blog posts per week that include those target keywords your ideal audience is searching for. These posts should be around 800-1,000 words, minimum.

- **Optimize your website for search engines.** Does your website load fast, or are your images a million megabytes? Have you optimized the alt-text for images and ensured your website is being crawled by search engines? You can hire someone to do all of these optimizations for you, or you can learn search engine optimization yourself. It's simple, but not easy. You'll have to do some research here to keep your site up-to-date depending on what website builder you've used.

- **Get relevant backlinks from other highly ranked sites.** Search engines want to know your content is poppin' off. How do they do that? By seeing if people on the Internet are linking back to your content. These "backlinks" give you bonus points and bump up your page ranking. The more backlinks to your site and pages, the higher your site appears on search. You can get these links from creating good content, getting others to share it, and also getting interviewed by journalists or other publications that can link to your website. The better ranked the site is that's linking to you, the more bonus points you get.

Be patient when you're building your blog: it can take up to three months for search engines to rank your new posts or pages, so this is a long-term strategy. For context, I'm still getting monthly visitors and jobs from posts I've published years ago.

Winning at the Web

Consider your freelancing website another part of your metaphorical garden: it takes time to grow, and you'll be pruning and watering it for years to come. If you're starting from scratch, know that your website will evolve with you and your career. If you pivot to a new niche or decide to hire a designer to help you rebrand, you may even redo your entire website in the future.

Don't worry about that now, though: do your best and keep consistent with your blog posts. Every piece of content you put out there is a new nugget of wisdom that will be out there on the Internet for a potential new client to find.

Keep planting seeds and you'll have a field of flowers in no time.

Amy's Field Notes: Blogging as Meditation

When I'm sitting down to write a blog, I need my cozy essentials by my side: a warm matcha latte sweetened with maple syrup, some coffeeshop music playing in the background, and a clean desk free of clutter and distractions.

My blogs aren't just helpful information: they're meant to be an opportunity for me to reflect on what I've learned or where I've been. Blogging is a form of meditation to me. I love the routine of opening up a blank post, picking the images, and curating how I share things with my readers.

I still get fan mail from my readers who have stumbled upon my posts or the knowledge I have to share, and it's great to hear from those who have found my ideas helpful. Vulnerability and transparency are key. That's how I build a rapport with my readers—and I hope you feel the same!

Don't just write on your blog: make a ritual out of it.

PART I: GETTING STARTED AS A FREELANCE WRITER

CHAPTER 10:
PROJECT TRACKING AND ENERGY MANAGEMENT

Time management is not going to save you.

Yes, these are the nuggets of wisdom you paid $15 for when you purchased this book, and yes, I do think this hot take will change your life. Here's why:

> You can't manage your time. Time is a finite source. But you can manage your energy and the strategy of how you approach projects—which, in turn, affects how much time you have.

If you think time-blocking and structured work sessions can get you to your income goals alone, I'd like to help you break some of your bad habits that your life before freelancing may have taught you.

Exit the 9-to-5 Matrix: Saying No to the Blue Pill Employee Life

Okay, I need to offer some words of tough love, because this is by far the biggest stumbling block that hurt me when I started as a freelancer:

I didn't unlearn my bad habits from my time of being an employee fast enough.

I was much like Neo, reluctant to fully understand the implications of

The Matrix and how my old life had kept me trapped.

When I skipped away from the world of clock-in-clock-out, full-time employment, I had a sense of gripping dread that whenever I wasn't at my desk between the hours of 9-to-5 I was ruining my career as a freelance writer. In fact, I overcompensated and spent a lot of time spinning my wheels instead of doing the things I *needed* to do.

I was working hard, *not* working smart.

That's why I burned out and nearly gave up on freelancing: I didn't have any strategy when it came to managing my *energy*.

Because here's the thing: the 9-to-5 industrial complex makes sense if most of that time is spent doing rote tasks to complete goals for someone else, sitting in meetings organized by other people, and not being productive for a large chunk of that day—but still collecting a paycheck just for being online and "available."

If you've made the leap and are a full-time freelance writer, it's important to break that habit of doing work for the sake of work. Now, you need to re-prioritize your time around what *actually* needs to get done—and throw out the rest.

Understand That Energy Management is Your Secret to Success

This is the secret sauce when it comes to finding success as a freelance writer.

First, let's look at the parts of freelance writing that can drain our energy faster than we'd like.

Energy draining activities as a freelancer:

- Difficult clients
- Complex projects without clear guidelines or expectations
- Poorly managed projects
- Juggling a large number of clients
- Work that you're not passionate about
- Fast turnarounds or unrealistic deadlines
- Low-paying assignments or clients
- Dealing with billing/bookkeeping/accounting work you could outsource

Some of these factors are out of our control, but some are controllable. If a client ends up being tough to work with and affecting your mood and productivity to the point where you're falling behind on your other work, it might be time to let them go—even if they pay well.

Same with the flip side: if you work for a really great client but they don't pay you well, you might need to move on if you're having trouble managing your workload and your other clients pay you better. Think back to the supply-and-demand section in Chapter Five.

The type of work you're doing matters, too. Once, I had a client who paid super well, and I could always expect an oversized paycheck from them every month. It was nice until I realized I dreaded the work I was doing. I found myself struggling to meet deadlines, and feeling exhausted every time I was working on that project. I ended up parting ways with that client—and the space I made was suddenly filled with work I was actually excited about, and ended up paying better, too!

In freelancing and in life, stay centered on your **true north**. Once you identify your true north, it's about doing the work needed to shift the sails and head in the direction you internally know you want to go. Don't be afraid: one twenty-minute hard conversation is better than months of unhappiness.

When you're freelance, you are… well… free to build the world you want around your priorities.

Freelancing takes a lot more work than a corporate job, but once you've traversed the forest of uncertainty, you're free to build a new home on land you've cultivated from scratch.

While it can be scary to turn down work or walk away from a lucrative assignment, pretty much every problem you encounter as a freelancer can be traced back to energy management. If you feel burned out consistently to the point where a day off isn't helping, then take a critical look at what makes you feel drained, and make adjustments to your projects from there.

Discomfort is the light that shines on what you need to overcome or change.

Prioritize Your "Green Light" Tasks and Habits

When it comes to energy management, this concept changed the way I looked at my schedule and how I prioritize things.

As a new freelancer, I spent too much time on the wrong things. I needed work, but instead of doing things that led to work (cold-emailing, outreach to potential clients, writing blogs on topics clients were searching for, submitting to jobs on freelancing platforms...) I was getting caught up in busywork. I was spinning my wheels, getting burned out and working eighty-hour weeks that were chaotic and I didn't understand why.

Now, I work a lot less—but get a lot more done!—and this is because I learned how to focus on my "Green Light" priorities.

Green Light priorities build momentum, and they directly lead to the outcome you want. Need clients? A Green Light priority would be to send ten cold emails per day. Have too many clients? A Green Light priority would be to redefine your pricing structure or understand how to outsource or scale.

"Yellow Light" activities are what I talked about earlier: things like writing on your blog or posting on social media. These things may get you clients (perhaps down the road when your blog is ranked or when your following has grown) but they aren't leading to a green-means-go moment *now*. You're still waiting at that intersection. There's nothing bad about having some Yellow Light things in your calendar: you do need to build up things like passive leads and income, but these shouldn't be the majority of your schedule, especially if you're feeling overwhelmed with clients or unsure where your next job is coming from. If things feel shaky in your world, it's usually best to divert energy from Yellow Light activities to Green Light activities and habits so you can see an immediate effect on your income and goals.

"Red Light" activities are true time-wasters: clients who can't afford you but want to hop on a call and try and haggle with you anyways, clients that are toxic or flaky, or even flat-out procrastination like endlessly scrolling through the Internet or watching TV instead of doing the work you need to get done. Red Light activities are actively sabotaging you, because they're not moments of true rest or learning experiences: they're time-wasters and energy black holes that suck the life out of you and can burn out freelancers who get caught up in this vicious cycle of Red Light distractions. If you want to find success, you need to eliminate Red Light tasks and clients ASAP so you're in a better headspace.

✷ Quick Tip: Color-Code Your Day

Want immediate feedback on how you're spending your time as a freelancer? Color-code your day using my Green Light, Yellow Light, and Red Light system. Designate all tasks that are directly related to your main goal right now as Green Light tasks. Place any non-priority tasks that can still help your business in the Yellow Light category. Give any toxic projects or mindless procrastination spirals a Red Light. Do this for a week. You can use a time-tracking tool to help you see how much time you spend doing certain things and sort them into different categories and colors. At the end of a week, look back at your schedule. How did you spend your time? What percentage were Green Light tasks that moved the needle? Are you still a bit shy of your goals, and do you need to devote more time to these types of tasks? What did your Yellow Light time look like? Are you building compounding projects in that time, or was that distracting you from your main priority? How did Red Light tasks sabotage you this week? No one else will audit your schedule, so it's up to you to take control of your time and energy!

Building Your Daily Schedule

I'll use my schedule as an example, but keep in mind, you'll need to experiment in order to find what works for you.

There's a concept known as Maker Days versus Manager Days that was popularized by Y-Combinator founder Paul Graham. Basically, it operates on the concept that we need to separate days in which we take meetings with days we focus on deep work.

Whether you're a CEO or a coder or a freelance writer, you need to block out spaces of at least **five uninterrupted hours of work time** in order to get in deep on a project. That's how you access a flow state and really make progress on a project.

I highly recommend coming up with a weekly schedule like one of the below:

- **M/W/F Maker Days, T/Th Manager Days:** Do you have a lot of long-term projects? Pick a schedule like this that corrals all your client meetings on Tuesday/Thursday so you have the rest of the workweek free. This is the schedule I usually opt for!

- **T/Th Maker Days, M/W/F Manager Days:** If you need to be more meeting-intensive or are on shorter-term projects, this might be a better schedule for you. Just be sure to protect your two maker days each week so you don't lose your precious work time.

Here's how I break down my daily routine on both maker days and manager days:

How I Spend My Manager (Meeting/Admin) Days:

8am-9am: Emails and First Calls. I don't have a set wake-up time, but I usually try and get up early enough to catch my European clients before their day ends if I'm working from the west coast. I start by making a matcha latte, answering emails, hopping on a quick call with said time zone dwellers, and prepping whatever I need to for the day. A lot of freelancers need morning time for deep focus, so pick the hardest set of admin tasks you need to clear and prioritize them first thing.

9am-noon: Admin Work, Brunch. If I can help it, I try not to schedule morning meetings. Instead, I try and clear any admin work. This could be following up on contracts or invoices, or it could be sending cold emails. Then, I'll finish up this time block with some brunch and maybe a morning meeting if one sneaks onto my calendar.

Noon-3pm: Meetings. When I can, I stack my meetings back-to-back in this sweet spot of the afternoon slump!

3pm-4pm: Workout + Coffee Break. Afternoon workouts are my favorite. At this point in my day, I need a break from my computer and need to venture out in the world for coffee and a hard workout. This could mean a trip to the gym, a pilates class, or just a walk around whatever city I'm in that week.

After my workout, I'm usually done for the day. I might shoot some content for my community, write a blog post, or cook dinner, but on manager days once my meetings are over it's usually time for me to rest. I don't do all my post-call follow-up work the same day: I usually save it for the next day as these calls can sometimes burn me out a bit as an introvert.

"But Amy, this schedule looks kinda like a 9-to-5?"

It does on paper, but in practice you'll find me cuddling up with a book some mornings, or skating out of my workday early to get a tour of Vatican City. Every day is a new adventure, and I get to choose how I spend it. The above schedule is to give you an idea, but I mold my day to my liking—and adjust it whenever I'm traveling!

If you're a newer freelancer, you might find these days stretch a bit longer as you rush to fill up your client roster. I prioritize a fifteen- to twenty-hour workweek (and it's taken time to get here!), so don't be discouraged if your schedule doesn't look quite like mine when you're starting off, you'll get there with time—if that's what you want!

How I Spend My Maker (Deep Work/Writing) Days:

I'll be honest, deep work days are my favorite. Meetings can be fun, but I much prefer the flow state of a writing day. (As a writer, that's to be expected!) I find these days to be cozy and nice because you can ignore your emails (since you handled the urgent ones the day prior on your admin day!), silence your phone, and just focus on the work ahead.

Here's what my schedule looks like these days:

8am-9am: Morning Routine. I wake up, journal, go on morning walk, and settle in for the day.

9am-noon: Deep Work and Writing Time. My favorite time of the week: deep work time! If I'm on a roll with a project, my writing time might stretch out for hours past this window.

Noon-1pm: Break. In the afternoon I take a break for food and a workout or an afternoon walk to reset.

1pm-3pm: Last Push. Before I hit my afternoon slump, I'll finish up the last writing work I'm in the middle of. Then, as my attention wanes, I'll maybe check my inbox or do some small admin tasks, but usually I'll just clock out after 2pm or 3pm hits.

Deep work days are nice because they're a true choose-your-own adventure and why I got into freelancing in the first place. Sometimes I write by the pool, or on a balcony overlooking the Amalfi Coast in Italy.

When people romanticize the life of a writer, days like this are why.

> ### ✴ Quick Tip: Clients Respect Policies, So Share Yours
>
> When I told clients that I would be taking Fridays off—forever—they respected my commitment to a four-day week. Having policies shows that you're a professional who knows their boundaries and can share them. These policies can be around four-day work weeks, business hours you're available, whatever helps you and your workflow. Any clients that question or disrespect your policies are clients you don't want to work with, so don't be afraid to be upfront with your policies!

How to Juggle Multiple Projects and Clients at Once

At any point in my freelancing career, I've been in the middle of between three and thirteen projects. These projects could be long-term memoir ghostwriting projects, or short-term blog posts. This isn't a flex, it's just a reminder that as a freelancer, you have to have multiple clients and projects. If you're only working on one project at a time, you're not a freelancer—you're an employee—and you are also not protecting yourself against the ups and downs of life and the economy. You *have* to have multiple projects at once—otherwise you will find yourself at the whims of your clients and their schedules, and you'll struggle to raise your rates if you don't have enough clients knocking down your door to hire you.

So, in order to manage all these different clients, you have to start by building your own client tracking system[5]. Any time you hop on a call with a client or begin a project with them, they should be added to some sort of list or spreadsheet. This is critical because I've had clients whom I've met with 2+ years ago for a free discovery call, and then, years later, they decide to work with me. Having notes from my original call helps me add an extra touch of personalization and share what I remembered from my original call with them.

But what happens when you're booked and busy (congrats!) and one of those leads lost to the wind comes back around and says "hey, are you free?"

---

5   Need help organizing your workflow? Find all my digital resources at: amysuto.com/six-figure-freelancer

Some freelancers have a "waitlist" and book clients a few weeks out. Others take on all the projects at once and adjust new project deadlines accordingly. If you're truly overrun with clients, that's a surefire sign your rates are too low and you need to increase them. You can also outsource or hire a small team of researchers and proofreaders to help you speed up your process, so it's up to you how you want to maximize your revenue.

It's okay to take on 20% more than you think you're capable of: clients often take time to get back to you, projects get delayed or canceled, and things go wrong. That 20% of extra work will help cushion any "down" weeks, and you may also realize that you can take on more work without destroying your schedule after all. But be careful of overcommitting beyond that limit: if you truly do end up drowning in work, all of your writing will suffer, and your clients will notice if you can't deliver the quality of work they're expecting from you.

Remember: this is a customer service business at the end of the day, so make sure you're managing your time and energy so that you can deliver great work while taking care of yourself!

Deadlines Are Not Your Friend

Don't set deadlines, set *timelines*.

Good:

I'd love to work with you on this project! Articles like these usually take me 3-5 business days to complete, with 2-3 days for revisions depending on what your notes are.

Bad:

I will deliver everything to you this Thursday by 5pm.

Let me explain: I know this is going to sound weird, but I try not to set deadlines. I'll give my clients estimates on when things are going to be done, but I don't set hard deadlines. In my head, I'll know what milestones I need to meet when, but I try not to communicate those specific days to my clients.

Why do I hate deadlines? No, it's not because I'm lazy. It's because of the aforementioned shuffling. My schedule is so fluid, and constantly shifting to accommodate all my different clients, life things, and other businesses. My clients hire me because I'm doing cool things—and it is sometimes those cool things that pull my attention away from my freelance work.

So, I try not to set deadlines, which helps my stress levels. That way, I don't feel like I'm failing, which keeps me in a positive mood, and ironically helps me finish things faster than if I did have deadlines. I have occasionally set aggressive deadlines when I thought I needed motivation to get a lot of work done quickly, but it's often backfired—leaving me burnt out or exhausted. In my opinion, it's better to work intuitively while keeping in mind your client's broader timeline, and then communicating with them along the way.

You'll need to figure out your own relationship to deadlines, but basically, if you have to set one, give yourself more time than you think you'll need. That way, you can deliver your work early in the best case, and on-time in the worst case.

I come from Hollywood where every production budget has something called contingency, which is usually 25% of what your budget is to account for all the things that are going to go wrong. If nothing goes wrong, congrats! There is 25% extra in the budget for creative production accounting to write-off later. Be a Hollywood production company: add a 25% contingency into any deadlines. You can't predict when things go wrong, but you can be prepared for them and that's what matters. Worst case scenario you did what you promised, best case you were even faster than the client expected.

Remember, if clients want you to constantly be available at a certain time or hit daily deadlines, they are most likely trying to shoehorn you into an employee role, not an independent contractor role. This is why you may need to gently remind certain clients that you've got other projects. If they wanted your exclusive attention, they'd hire you as an employee with a full-time salary.

Assuming neither of you want or are able to have that relationship, they'll need to understand why you have to stay flexible. There are even laws about this in certain states when it comes to the classification of freelancer versus employee: an employee is required to be somewhere at a certain time, and a freelancer sets their own schedule (or some verbiage similar to this.) As a freelancer, your clients need to know you've got to keep up a bunch of other projects and clients to pay the bills.

Short-Term vs. Long-Term Projects and Clients

When you're building your client base, it's important to try and find the right balance of short-term and long-term clients.

Long-term clients are great because you can build fruitful working relationships with awesome people, and you'll be able to get into a rhythm of knowing how to work well together.

On the other hand, if you make a long-term commitment that you can't or don't want to keep, it can be uncomfortable to disentangle yourself after your clients have already gone down the road with you. There's less flexibility with long-term clients, and if you have to pass up other opportunities because of the amount of bandwidth the long-term clients take, you may find yourself in a tough spot if your long-term client ends their working relationship with you and you need to scramble to fill in the gaps. However, long-term clients are a key part of your freelance business, because the amount of time it takes to find and onboard a new client can be inefficient. This is one of the reasons I got into memoir writing: I work for clients for months at a time, which means I know I'll have steady work.

Short-term projects like blog posts are much more start-and-stop, and it's harder to predict your workload and plan and budget accordingly. Shorter projects also afford a kind of flexibility that long-term projects don't have: you're able to hop on and off projects more easily, and it's no big deal if you end up not having availability or interest on a short-term project. It's more of a hassle to find and vet new clients, so you'll need to charge a bit more with a short-term project because there's a good amount of unpaid time you'll need to spend finding and interviewing for these projects.

As a freelancer, you'll want a mix of both short-term and long-term projects to reduce risk and be able to pay your bills without giving up your independence. The more clients you work with, the more your risk is spread out across all of your clients: chances are, they're not all going to leave you at the same time.

Let's break it down in terms of your time and money:

A **larger writing project** like a set of foundational copy deliverables might net you $50,000 total, but will take you ten hours per week for sixteen weeks to complete. That breaks down to **$3,125 per week**. I'll get into optimizing your fixed-rate package rates later in this book, so you can further optimize your time and work fewer hours!

A **medium-sized writing project** like a landing page can net established freelance writers anywhere from **$5,000 or more per project**, which can be easily done alongside your month of long-term projects.

A **small writing project** might be a flat rate of **$600 per blog post** or other small deliverable, which takes you two to three hours of work as you become a more efficient writer.

For this setup, the best division of projects might be **two long-term projects at twenty hours per week which comes out to $25,000 for the month, and then you've got five hours left over for taking on medium or small writing projects as they come up to keep you at a twenty-five-hour work week.** Add five more hours per week for admin work, and you've got thirty hours per week of freelancing at your most busy.

In terms of money, that's approximately **$30,000/month** before taxes, just for the mix-and-match of the above projects.

And that's it: that's the math you need to make a healthy six-figure year as a freelance writer where you're making **$360,000 before taxes**.

Not bad for a starving artist, eh?

Setting Boundaries and Enjoying Your Free Time

When you're a full-time freelancer, your clients will assume you're just doin' your 9-to-5 hustle and hanging out at your desk waiting for them to call. Some clients will know you're managing other clients, but still probably don't understand the kind of bandwidth juggling multiple clients takes. Still others will expect you to work weekends or weeknights. When you get a call at 9pm on a Saturday from a client who wants to chat about your project—well, that's not okay. (Unless you're okay with working that late on a weekend, but if you are, you may want to consider giving yourself another day off during the week.)

Before all that, though, you need to iron out your project tracking board, and get organized so you don't get overwhelmed. Then, you can start creating boundaries and communicating those with clients while still being sufficiently available to them so you can complete your work and collaborate with your clients effectively.

The nice thing about working freelance? I've been able to travel the world and enjoy the view at the Riegrovy Sady Park overlooking Prague (a great place for a date and a picnic while you watch the sunset!) I can go on a hike at 11am on a Wednesday and it won't be busy. I can book a flight without having to check in with a supervisor or request time off.

The downside? I'm often working on weekends or odd hours to catch up on things I didn't get to during the week if I've been jet setting, or if a particularly busy week snuck up on me. Also, most airplanes have Wi-Fi, so a travel day can be a good catch-up day if you plan it right. Business class can be seen as a slightly more expensive, chic co-working space.

No matter what, remember this: the work will never end. Your to-do list will never be empty. The only thing that will end is your capacity to do it. Practice finding balance now: your body and mind (and bank account!) will thank you later!

Amy's Field Notes: How to Protect Your Energy

"Can we push this meeting to later this afternoon?" a founder asked me over email. I was working with them on a project, and it was a Thursday. I did *not* want to push a morning meeting to the afternoon. Was I busy that Thursday afternoon? No, but I knew I wouldn't be in the best mood if I took the call, and I had been pushing myself hard at that time to overdeliver for that project.

"Sorry, that doesn't work. But here are some times that work for me next week!" I replied, and sent over my calendar link with more times. The people pleaser inside of me threw a tantrum, wanting to just say yes and accommodate everyone—but that's what burned me out in the first place in previous years.

Protecting your energy can be scary: especially when we're so used to the hustle culture go-go-go. It can feel weird to give yourself Fridays off for your own creative projects rather than just grinding away for the machine.

But, in reality, you're doing your clients a favor. By protecting your energy, you show up happier and do better work. You give them a better return on their investment by taking care of yourself and giving your work the room it needs to breathe.

Being kind to yourself is good for business.

PART I: GETTING STARTED AS A FREELANCE WRITER

CHAPTER II:
HANDLING DIFFICULT SITUATIONS WITH CLIENTS

I joke sometimes that being a freelance writer can feel—at times!—like you're a coffee shop barista, just with more complicated orders from your customers.

As someone who has worked service jobs before, I can say with absolute certainty that being a freelance writer is superior to every other job I've ever had. I've been a Hollywood assistant, a Resident Advisor (RA), and a front desk reception worker at a post-production lab. In those jobs, I was paid near minimum wage, dealt with people often facing difficult days in their lives who would take it out on me, and couldn't wear my PJs to work. As a freelance writer, I have the flexibility to turn down clients, pick my projects, and work from home—all while being paid hundreds of thousands of dollars more than I did as a minimum-wage worker.

However, freelancing in all forms is still a customer service job. You *can* say yes if someone comes to you wanting a complicated half-caf Pumpkin Spiced Latte with two shots of vanilla syrup and sweet cream foam because they are absolutely delightful to work with. But sometimes when you're trying to make a simple cold brew it might end up being a bit of a nightmare if your customer is a grump and they realize they *meant to say* they wanted an Americano—and now they're refusing to pay for their first drink despite it being what they initially ordered.

I've worked with the full spectrum of clients, and I've been in customer service hell a number of times. Sometimes, things have turned out okay and I've saved the project, and other times, I've had to lean into my contract with the client to protect me as I stepped away and closed things out.

Let's break down some of the situations that might come up so you can learn from my mistakes and be prepared if something goes wrong.

Scenario #1: Client is Unhappy with Your Work

As I've mentioned many times in this book, I'm a recovering people pleaser. What can I say? I'm an ambitious eldest daughter. I'm also human: I like to be accepted for who I am and for people to love the work I do for them. As a professional freelance writer, I've been lucky to see that a majority of my clients do dig my work, but it wasn't always that way.

Early on in my career as a freelance writer, I was still learning how to best work with people and deliver what they were looking for. I was also a new copywriter, still learning as I grew. Confidence in your work grows slowly over time, and you have to put in the hours to learn and improve with every job.

Whether you're an expert or brand-new freelance writer, you're not going to knock every assignment out of the park. Trust me: it's not possible.

If a client doesn't like the work you turn in, set your ego aside and turn on your customer service personality. Diagnose what went wrong, validate your client's feelings—they are hiring you to help them, after all—and set forth a plan to make things right. Some bumpiness is normal if you're just starting with a client and trying to capture what they want on the page, so really listen to what they're saying and do your best in the rewrite phase. If you've exhausted all your rewrites and they're still not happy, consider offering a complimentary revision.

However, if your client is acting rude and not respecting you, just finish out your contract and walk away. You're a professional, after all, and you deserve to be treated like one by your clients. You also don't want to be in business with people who blow up at you or who can't control their emotions or communicate clearly.

Scenario #2: Client Refuses to Pay or Client's Company Goes Bankrupt

Sometimes, it's payday and the client's company is dead and gone. RIP. And you can do... pretty much nothing.

There are legal channels you can pursue, of course: check in with your lawyer to see what's possible based on the amount owed, the language in your contract, and local laws and regulations.

In many scenarios, however, it will cost you more money in legal fees to recover an unpaid invoice than the sum of that invoice.

This is why it is absolutely *essential* to get an upfront deposit from your client. That way if they ghost you, you still have half of the payment already in your account. Check with your CPA, but you may also be able to write-off the unpaid invoice on your taxes and save some money on your tax bill.

When I have clients who are late to pay their invoices, I stay on my reminders with the invoice (I have an automated software that helps to remind my clients of any late invoices so it's not coming from me, personally), and usually it gets paid. Your lawyer may also advise you to include a late fee for unpaid invoices, so that the late payment accrues interest until it's paid. I've also had clients whose startups have closed or gone bankrupt before they could pay me.

This is yet another reason why you need to charge enough so that one or two unpaid invoices isn't going to crater your entire freelance business. Remember, as a freelancer you take on more risk than employees, which is why you also need to charge more!

Scenario #3: Client Asks You to Work Beyond the Scope of Your Agreement

I've found that sometimes clients just don't read my emails or the contract they've signed—even if we've discussed the details in-depth on a call.

I was in the middle of doing a full rewrite on a draft when this happened: I had to (gently!) remind the client that we had exceeded the number of rewrites when they asked me for another round of edits. I offered to do a polish with some proofreading changes, but let them know that to do any deep changes, I'd need to close out our contract and work hourly. The client was confused, and I had to point to the contract and past discussions we'd had. The client paid the final invoice but didn't move forward with me on an hourly basis. It was a clean break, but sometimes it's not always this way.

I've also had clients who I've had to remind that our contract terms have been exceeded, and they valued my work and were happy to switch to an hourly contract.

Be kind but firm in your email to your client.

> ### ✸ Quick Template: Out-of-Scope Deliverable
>
> For reference, here's a template of what I usually send, but be sure to chat with your lawyer if you need guidance on how to enforce your contract:
>
> *Hey [Client]!*
>
> *I've loved working with you on [this freelance project.] I just wanted to let you know that we've [exceeded our number of rewrites/this request is beyond the scope of our initial agreement]. I'd be happy to [finish up this rewrite/complete any small notes you may have on this draft/any other small concession you may want to offer or work you can wrap up] but if you'd like me to continue on this project, we'll need to [re-scope our contract/switch to an hourly contract].*
>
> *I've enjoyed working with you so far on this project, so would love to know how you'd like to move forward!*
>
> *Best,*
> *[your name]*

Scenario #4: Dealing with Disorganized Founders or Teams

There was this freelance project I was *so* excited about. I was working on a fixed-rate fee and doing a mix of creative copywriting, and the company was a hot startup with in-person creative events. I was thrilled to be on the team, but from the jump, it was clear there were some problems and drama within the team.

I was hired by the founders, and cleared my scope of work with them before I signed the contract. When I started working on a day-to-day basis, however, I realized that the new department head I was working with had no idea what my scope of work was. I sent this department head my job description, and found myself doing work way beyond my contract. I was also in hours and hours of meetings per week—something that is a rarity as a freelancer, as I usually work with teams organized enough to work asynchronously rather than requiring weekly meetings.

So, I had to stop the presses. I paused my contract and met with the founders. They were annoyed that I had stopped attending meetings, but I had to explain that we were dealing with a scope issue, and I had to go back to the basics of getting the department head himself to outline the work he needed from me, and from there, I had to generate a brand-new statement of work and quote for my work.

To be honest, the entire process was frustrating, especially as I was working with the team's contract instead of my own. I had accepted the project because I was dazzled by the potential of the company, and in doing so had also signed myself up for a tricky situation within their team.

After hopping on several calls with different team members, I managed to smooth out our disagreement, create a new scope of work and a better system, and continued working with the team—and things got much better.

Not every conflict has a "happily ever after." There are going to be assignments that come your way as a freelancer that seem flashy and fun, and you're going to want to waive your due diligence and let your boundaries relax so you can fit into the team and get the job.

Don't.

Anytime I've accepted a job at a lower rate or let my boundaries relax for a project that I justified as fun or a good portfolio item, I regretted it.

You never know what's below the surface of a project or a team, which is why you need to make sure you're protected. Just like a deep-sea diver, you need your equipment to protect you from what's underneath. As a freelancer, your equipment is your contract and your ability to set expectations and stand by your boundaries—this keeps your bank account breathing.

Scenario #5: The Project Extends Longer Than Anticipated

I learned fast that some fixed-rate projects will extend into infinity and beyond unless you give your clients deadlines to turnaround notes on your work.

Let's say I hire you, an amazing freelance writer, to write a manifesto for my healthy, Christian-faith-based breakfast cereal, Praisen Dan. Very cool! I pay you half upfront of your $5,000 fee to commence work, and you turn in an awesome manifesto that lives up to the Praisen Dan name that any son of Jacob would be proud of… Okay, enough of the Bible puns. I email you saying "this is great! I'll get back to you with notes" and then I disappear. We have two optional rewrites in your contract—but no end date or contingencies on when those rewrites could or should take place.

Two years later, I resurface and I'm like "hey there! I have notes on this cereal manifesto you wrote two years ago" and you may be contractually obligated to finish up those notes before I release payment to you.

This is another great thing to talk to your lawyer about, and something to potentially include in your contract depending on your lawyer's advice.

I've had hourly contracts extend for three or four years because of the same reason, but I actually don't mind those! If a client blips in and out but they still pay me my hourly rate when I invoice them, all's good and merry in my mind.

It's the fixed-rate jobs that cause issues, because there's a second payment just in the wind that may never come due unless I account for that in my contract.

In summary? Use these scenarios to pressure test your contract to make sure you're covered in many different cases (that all happened to me!)

Scenario #6: Client Is or Becomes Mentally Unwell

On two occasions, I've had to end contracts with clients who I realized were mentally unwell. When you're working with individuals (and not companies) you roll the dice a bit, especially in the memoir ghostwriting space. I've written memoirs for many amazing, thoughtful people, but occasionally, narcissists and people experiencing delusions hire me and I don't realize the extent of their illness or narcissism until we're well along our journey.

This is part of the reason why I only work for an hourly rate in the memoir space these days: an hour worked is an hour paid, regardless of where we are in the process. That way, I can hand over any work I've done if I need to cancel the contract and walk away for any reason.

If you think your client is potentially unstable, you need to cancel your contract with them *now*. As a freelancer, you have to protect yourself. There are dangerous people in the world, and while they probably won't do anything to harm you, you still need to take precautions. Depending on the situation, you may also need to hide the real reason you're ending the contract. You can discuss with your lawyer, as they'll be more familiar with the cancellation terms on your contract, but personally, I've told clients that my chronic illness is requiring me to cancel the contract, or I need to take some time off for personal reasons and kept it vague. (I've also legitimately ended contracts where my health or personal reasons prevented me from continuing, so it's important that you have space in your contract to end a working relationship for these reasons!)

This is also why it's critical to have a PO box address that you use for receiving mail or for putting on your contracts. By working remotely, you've already got a layer of protection, but you still need to be careful. I don't want you to be afraid or paranoid, of course: even in heated situations I've walked away from, nothing bad has happened.

At the end of the day, use common sense and always listen to your gut. Don't work with clients who creep you out or make you feel weird: there are so many amazing clients out there who won't drain your energy or make you feel like something's off.

Scenario #7: Client or Company Requests Too Many Meetings

Another reason why I like to work hourly is to protect against the scourge that is the meeting-that-should-have-been-an-email.

Listen, I love human interaction as much as everyone else. But what I *don't* love is when I'm roped into huge video calls that don't require my presence and cut into my deep work time. As a freelancer, I'm not paid for these unless I'm an hourly freelancer (in which case I'll be in whatever meetings you want me to be in!), and so, if you're on a fixed-rate contract, you have to include a maximum number of meetings so you don't get treated like an employee without being compensated properly.

Even with my hourly clients, I encourage asynchronous work whenever possible—that is, working on a flexible schedule with tools like email, voice memos, and other collaboration tools that don't require my client and I to be on a call at the same time (and aligning our schedules like traditional synchronous workplaces we all are used to!) When I was four years into freelancing, I finally started encouraging my clients to use voice memos and screenshare recordings in lieu of meetings, and it's changed the entire way I approach projects.

I've ghostwritten entire memoirs simply by exchanging voice memos with my client and not hopping on calls for months at a time, proving that most Zoom calls can be communicated in different ways. This is especially true because I'm usually in a different time zone than my client, and I'm also juggling other projects and clients.

If your clients refuse to accommodate your schedule, it might be time to move on from working with them. One of the key legal definitions of being a freelancer is that we need to be able to work with our own tools on our own schedule. If they want you to attend every company meeting, they should probably hire a full-time employee instead.

When to Give Refunds or a Money-Back Guarantee

Every freelancer has a different policy when it comes to giving refunds. Personally, I don't offer refunds or any refund guarantee. I ask my clients to take the risk of working with me, and provide a hefty portfolio and hundreds of reviews from happy clients to convince them. I used to have clients balk at my high rates, but once I established a trusted track record, more people were happy to sign on and work with me.

That doesn't mean I don't take client satisfaction seriously: in fact, I try to offer clients many touchpoints to give feedback on the direction of the project, and often create a detailed project proposal at the start of a job for the client to review before I even put pen to paper on the project itself.

Great communication is key to this: I'm able to parse through and understand exactly what clients want, understanding both said and unsaid directions.

But if you're a new freelancer still figuring it out, it's up to you if you want to offer a money-back guarantee. I don't recommend it, as I think instead you should just price your rates a bit lower and build up to a higher rate with every glowing review. Just know that any sort of refund or money-back guarantee puts the risk on *you*, the freelancer—even if the client is in the wrong for their lack of communication or if they don't really understand what they need.

So, if you're going to give a refund, provide it if *you're* in the wrong or if you need to end a project early. Otherwise, stick to your guns: they hired you, and if you don't work out, politely end the contract and refer the client to another freelancer in your network. *Pew Pew.*

A Client is Always Right, But Maybe Not Right for You

Your clients are always right, but they may not be right for you.
You can find better, so don't let a scarcity mindset stop you. That said, when (and how) should you cut ties with a client?

As a freelancer, your reputation is important. If you've made a commitment to a client, finish out the project. It's best to follow through and then end your working relationship when your commitment naturally comes to an end, and you're also likely bound by a contract and are obligated on the legal side of things to see it through, anyways. A project is like a voyage across the ocean: stopping halfway isn't really an ideal option for either side, but once you hit port you can change ships.

However, sometimes a project is dead-on-arrival and the boat is sinking before you even set sail. You might sign a contract and then get ghosted, or your client might have unreasonable expectations or an unclear vision for what they think they want. If you're taking on water early in the process, you're probably going to want to finish out the work and end the contract before your boat swims with the fishes.

The few times I've had to end a project prematurely turned out okay in the end: I articulated what I was observing with my client ("it seems like we're not on the same page" or "it doesn't look like I'm the right writer for what you're wanting here") and we came to a decision together and amicably parted ways. A few of these clients even left me nice reviews because I didn't continue to just take their money: I was trying to protect them as much as I wanted to make sure I was set up for success on my end. The captain always goes down with their ship, but if you're close to harbor, you can always go find a new boat before that's the case.

There are rare cases in which you might find yourself working with a toxic client who doesn't respect you. In those cases, drop them and run like the wind. Try and do so with as much grace and kindness as possible, but also don't allow yourself to get entangled with people who don't treat you well.

At the end of the day, trust your gut and do the best you can. Your gut will learn as you gain experience. If you have any reservations about working with someone—SAY NO. Every time I've ignored this feeling, I've regretted it. Freelancing should be a positive and rewarding experience: don't work with people who don't respect you and your work.

Amy's Field Notes: Set Aside Your Ego

Earlier this year, I was writing some web copy for a startup. For the sake of confidentiality, let's say this startup was a jetpack manufacturer called Sky's the Limit and the CEO's name was Chip.

Chip sent me a brief, and I did thorough research on their competitors. I created a proposal for the copy I was going to write for their landing page. Chip loved my proposal, and I started on the landing page.

However, when I turned in the landing page, Chip thought the direction felt a little too witty and light. He didn't love the tagline *Let's Get Packin'!* even though that was in my initial brief he signed off on.

I told Chip I wanted him to love the copy I wrote for him. What notes did he have for me so I could take another pass? Chip sent me some new notes, but I had a feeling it contradicted all of the initial brand work I did for him. His notes were trying to make Sky's the Limit some stuffy, serious brand, and they were selling *jetpacks* for goodness' sake. However, I set my ego aside and turned in a rewritten page incorporating Chip's ideal tone.

When Chip read my new version, he sent me a thank you note. "Hey Amy, thanks for your gritty reboot for this copy! It looks great. Upon discussion with the team, we realized that your first pass was actually more in line with what our voice is. We're going to go with that instead, but I appreciate you doing the rewrite as I know it was probably against your better judgment. Would love to work with you again on another assignment!"

The lesson here? Jetpacks are meant to be fun. Oh, and your client is always right—even if they're not.

I could have stomped my feet and pointed out the obvious, but that wouldn't have won me more chips with Chip. He probably didn't consult his team when he gave me his revision notes, so he was wanting to test out a brand voice that wasn't aligned with the direction his team was going in. I brought my A-Game to his revision request, and he thanked me for it even after he realized my first pass was exactly what he wanted.

This is also why you have to include these potential curveballs into your fixed-rate projects. You need to give the client wiggle room to feel out the direction they want to go, and understand that it may change as they discover what they want—and don't want.

Check your ego at the door and approach every job with an open mind, as that's the recipe to a robust list of returning clients. I mean, sky's the limit when you do.

PART I: GETTING STARTED AS A FREELANCE WRITER

CHAPTER 12:
EXPLORING DIFFERENT FREELANCE WRITING TYPES

When you're starting to dabble in different freelance types and niches, you'll come across a number of different forks in the road. A client might ask you if you do copywriting in addition to blog writing. You might feel like your narrative story structure can lend itself to writing memoirs.

While there are many skews of freelance writing (travel writing, beauty blogging, journalistic writing—you name it!) I'm going to go over some of the most profitable ones below. That doesn't mean that something I don't cover here *isn't* profitable—these are just the freelance writing niches I've personally had experience in that I can speak to as viable, high-earning options.

So, if you're curious about different types of freelance writing or want to expand your offerings or switch your niche, this chapter is for you.

Picking the Right Freelance Work for You

Finding the right categories of freelance writing is important in order to really work in an area that plays to your strengths.

For example, I love memoirs because I love listening to people and asking them questions about their life. I also love long-term projects because I like to get to know my clients on a personal level and really help them dive into their life stories.

Think about what your ideal workday would look like, and then build an alchemy of freelance work around that. If you love hopping from client to client and chatting with a variety of people at a variety of different companies, maybe copywriting might be better for you. If you prefer digging in deeper with fewer clients and having less calls, maybe developmental editing/memoir ghostwriting is for you.

Keep an open mind and don't be afraid of a learning curve!

How to Write a Memoir as a Ghostwriter

Memoir ghostwriting is one of my favorite formats. I love crafting a narrative around people's stories, and sending them clever questions so they can respond through voice memos. If you also have a natural curiosity about people's lives, this could be a great niche for you. (If not, maybe pick a different niche!)

Generally, here's what the memoir process entails:

- Getting to know your client.
- Deep research and background: interviewing your client and their family, reading anything related to their story, and formulating timelines on major life events.
- Writing an entire rough draft of a book (!!!) sometimes with the help of a writer's assistant to make sure your notes stay organized and you don't miss important details.
- Interviewing your client on a weekly basis as you write the book, or have them send you voice memos with content to include in the book.
- Rewriting the book with your client's notes and the notes of any beta readers.
- Proofreading/polishing the book and finalizing the manuscript.

Memoir ghostwriting is a profitable niche at the higher levels, but you have to charge enough to make writing a whole book worth your time. Ghostwriting books is energy-intensive, so make sure your rates reflect that.

How to Write Creative Copy as a Copywriter

Copywriting is a lucrative but challenging field, with great lessons to teach us as writers. If you're looking to learn how to be economical with words, this path offers a great way to learn.

In my experience with copywriting, here are the skills you'll need to hone:

- Be able to understand how to establish or mimic their "brand voice."
- Understand how to turn boring, technical copy into a bangin' party.
- Distill complex, utterly convoluted information into an easy-to-understand website homepage or newsletter or whatever.
- Sell products like it's an art form and wax poetic about candles or whatever your client is selling.
- Understand your client's mission and help them communicate it to the world. The most important part of writing great copy is to accurately understand what your client is trying to convey.
- Active listening is a critical component of copywriting. It is for any freelance job, but with copywriting, you are operating in a sort of Sherlockian capacity trying to understand the heart of what your client is trying to say and then being the one to help them say it.

Copywriting pays really well if you're great at it, but it might take some swings and misses to really be able to hone in on your deliverable. Be super generous with your early clients, and offer more rewrites for free if they're not satisfied. The more copy you write, the better you'll get at nailing a company's voice on the first try.

If you have a creative background, you can apply storytelling principles to copywriting: think of copy and brand voices as if they were a character in itself. How will this "character" communicate best with a target audience? How can you speak to people so they will actually listen? How can you keep your messaging concise?

I love the book *Building a StoryBrand* by Donald Miller[6]. It's a great distillation of how to weaponize great copy to help your clients sell their products or services.

---

6   For more book recommendations, visit: amysuto.com/six-figure-freelancer

How to Write Social Media and Newsletter Copy

From captions to video scripts to ghostwriting for writing-forward platforms, copywriting for social media platforms is an art in itself.

Social media and newsletter copywriting might feel pretty small if you're an outsider looking in, but in reality, this field is filled with busy professionals who need ghostwriters to help them keep up the content they need to put out on a regular basis.

Going viral and building an audience is a prerequisite for everything these days. Want to sell tie-dye onesies? Improve your status as an investor who only invests in carbon-neutral pet products? You'll need an audience for that. And how do you amass a large following? You need content.

Every video starts off with a script and an idea. Every newsletter requires pithy, concise recaps of current events. This content doesn't come from nowhere: great writers make this stuff up.

Just know if you dive into the social media space, your clients will also expect you to be in-the-know with the latest trends and what's winning on the algorithm side of things. If you don't *eat, sleep, and breathe* the Internet every day, this ain't the job for you. But if you want to turn your addiction into a career and love writing short, attention-grabbing hooks and content, this could be the right path for you.

Signs You've Picked the Right Type of Freelance Writing

So, you've picked a format, you've started booking jobs, and you want to know: have I picked the right type of freelance writing for me?

Here are some things to consider:

- Do I enjoy waking up every day and writing about this thing?
- Am I curious when I'm on client calls, and do I feel compelled to ask them questions both for the project and for my own interest?
- Am I generally energized by this work?
- Do I enjoy doing my own research about this subject and reading about it?
- Do the clients in my niche pay well for freelance writers and value the written word?

If you answered "no" for more than one of the above questions, you may want to keep looking for a niche that fits you. Remember: passion is the secret sauce here. Without passion, you'll lose out on jobs to people who actually care about this stuff. And life is short—why do something you're not enjoying?

Amy's Field Notes: Staying on the Cutting Edge

I became a TV writer five years too late. As I was studying at USC, the TV bubble had burst, directors and film auteurs had rushed to take the reins, and the writers-assistant-to-staff-writer ladder had broken down.

I missed that boat, but that allowed me to be the first to jump on the cutting edge of a brand-new industry: web3.

When I realized the incredible role that creative writers and other artists were playing in the advent of web3, I saw a huge opportunity to shape the future of media and storytelling. So, I started packing my schedule with web3 conferences, I dove all-in on innovative, immersive projects centering around AR and VR, and rode the wave to the top of my field, fast.

I redid my portfolio, leaned hard into my past work with startups to get web3 assignments, and redid my cover letters and website with a web3 focus front-and-center, with package pricing options geared towards people looking to launch NFT collections or web3 startups.

As a freelance writer, you have a lot more flexibility to pivot to a new field or industry. You can try out a new niche while still keeping your primary focus on your old niche.

With that said, you still need a track record of great work in order to be able to dive into a new niche: don't lose focus on making sure you're always turning in high-quality writing!

PART 1: GETTING STARTED AS A FREELANCE WRITER

CHAPTER 13:
COMMON SPELLING AND GRAMMAR MISTAKES THAT FREELANCE WRITERS MAKE

Look, I get it: nobody became a writer to agonize over comma placement and capitalization rules.

But, if you're getting paid for your work, everything you turn in should be polished and be held to the highest standards of the English language. Even if your client doesn't know every nuance of grammar rules, they'll be able to feel if something doesn't read the way it should.

I've compiled this list of the most common mistakes I've seen across the board when it comes to the written word. Consider this my addendum to Strunk & White's *Elements of Style*[7]. (Which, if you haven't read, you absolutely should! A phenomenal and short book on all things about writin' gud.)

As a disclaimer before we dive in: these rules apply specifically to projects done in the United States, as different countries have their own style guides.

Cool? Let's dive in.

---

7   For more book recommendations, visit: <u>amysuto.com/six-fig-ure-freelancer</u>

Improper Use of Semicolons

God, I hate semicolons. I use them once in a blue moon, but generally I think they're pretty useless compared to the rest of the punctuation in our collective literary arsenal. If you must use them, please oh please use them right because they stand out like a sore thumb when they're misplaced.

Semicolons separate two **independent clauses**, which means if you covered up the semicolon with your thumb, the two halves of your sentence would be full, complete sentences on their own.

This is a good semicolon usage example; we are happy with this semicolon usage even though a colon would have been better.

But the things I feel; when the first half of this sentence is a dependent clause that can't be interrupted by a semicolon because it would be a sentence fragment on its own. This is exactly how a semicolon **shouldn't** be used.

Em Dash vs. En Dash

Dashes—what amazing things they are. I love the way dashes help my eyes dart over the page, they're great for pacing. But did you see the dash I used at the top of this paragraph? To get that typed perfectly, you'll notice that I hit the dash key twice and did not put a space on either end. That's an **em dash**, and what we typically think of when we think of a dash used as a punctuation tool.

An en dash is used in hyphens and ranges, like I worked out from 3pm-4pm today. That's an en dash. (Also notice: no spaces on either side.) You only hit the dash key once for these.

If you're a screenwriter, you probably write your dashes like this:

"And then — she RAN TOWARD THE TRACTOR PARTY, barreling down the Nashville Music City street — and she didn't miss the party!!!"

Party tractors aside, we *looooooove* to abuse dashes in screenwriting. We also put spaces on either end because it looks better in screenwriting software.

Internet articles also have em dashes with spaces on each side. Same with pretty much every single other format except for manuscripts. But in manuscript format, dashes hold on tight to the words around them. Don't give them room to breathe!!! Suffocate those bad boys with ink!!!

Capitalization Inconsistencies

Did you know that if you mention your Mom or Dad in a sentence they should be capitalized because you're referring to a specific person and not some random mom or dad from the Mom and Dad store?

In addition: the first word after a colon is NOT capitalized.
For example: Not this.

(I know there's some debate on this one, so I'm siding with the Chicago Manual of Style on this one. Unless you're using APA's style guide, follow the above rules!)
I'm not going to get too far down the road with this one, but basically if you're capitalizing something, ask yourself *"why?"* If you're not, also ask yourself *"why?"* And that's a great way to become the insane asylum's best grammar whiz :)

Getting "Weird" with Quotation Marks

"What did quotations ever do to us?" I asked, staring at my computer in awe about how many ways they seemed to be creatively used.

No:
"Things that are "quoted.""

Yes:
"You can use baby 'quotes.'"

No:
"Why are you putting the question mark outside the quotation"?

Yes:

"Why aren't you putting it inside the quotation marks like this?"

No:
"Where did that exclamation mark go"!

Yes:
"All punctuation goes within quotation marks where it belongs!"

No:
"But what if I want to hoard ALL 'the punctuation'?".

Yes:
"No."

Always run spell check or whatever your tool of choice is! Technology is here to help us, so lean on the tools that help you! If clients are seeing spelling errors that could have been caught by a robot, they'll wonder why you didn't just use the robot.

Why We're So Tense About Tense

Tense issues are the number one problem I see in new writers' work. Unless there's a very good reason to do so, all memoirs and most book projects should be in past tense.

As a screenwriter who has also written things for the Internet, I know we use present tense to create a sense of immediacy for first-person articles and as a matter of necessity for screenwriting.

However, in books it feels very odd for the reader—especially in a reflective memoir—to break into present tense. I think it's in part because of the form: a book feels a lot less immediate than a blog article. For memoirs, this is particularly relevant because we're already in a space to hear a retelling of someone's life, so the present tense shift feels particularly jarring.

The worst thing you can do is jump from present tense to past tense and have inconsistencies throughout, so make sure that you're staying consistent.

Not Capturing Voice or Sounding Too Formal

For most types of writing, you're going to write in a more conversational style. Sure, it's an ~elevated~ conversation with a lot more imagery and cool stuff, but at the end of the day, if you're writing in someone's voice it should feel like that.

For example, I have a ton of contractions throughout this document. Often, I get chapters back where people write things like "he did not know where he was to go next" instead of "he didn't really know where to go next."

See how big of a change some contractions make? Some of the best writing has the feel of a conversation but the impact of a revelation: it's all about putting care into how you're constructing the book.

Sentence and Paragraph Flow Tips

The fundamentals of what makes a flowing sentence are more important than you think. Even the selection of consonants makes a difference: I chose the word "flowing" above because I liked how it felt with "fundamentals." See what I mean? You'll also notice that every sentence in this paragraph is a different length. The variation makes it feel interesting, and keeps your attention in a way that doesn't feel repetitive or like I'm just listing things in paragraph form.

In prose, it's important you're studying what makes for an impactful, meaty paragraph. That begins with the skill of building memorable turns of phrase, but adds up to the imagery and impact of full paragraphs.

Most documents and blogs out there have short, tense paragraphs. The Internet has taught us to write that way, and if you're writing content for the world wide web, that makes total sense. But if you're writing a paragraph for a book, the feeling of the sentences should be a lot different. I can't break all of the nuances down in this chapter, but the best way to really hone your fundamental skills in prose is just to read more.

Formatting for Book Projects

Manuscripts have their own witchcraft, which I encourage you to look up on the Internet to walk through all the specifics.

One major mistake I see is this: make sure you're using **page breaks** when starting new chapters, not just indents. Otherwise, if you're just hitting enter, if someone pops your file into a different word processor or goes into edit it, the chapter breaks won't stick and they'll spill into each other. Also—don't forget your page numbers!

Basically, you want your document to be as clean and beautiful on the page as possible. You want your client to see only the things they love, not any of the other stuff.

If a typo slips past your radar, that's no big deal. It's more that when you're perpetually misusing something, nobody is gonna tell you. They'll just be able to know when something isn't quite right with what's on the page, even if they can't articulate what. And that could be the difference between retaining clients—or not.

At the end of the day, if proofreading/grammar stuff makes you hate your life, consider subcontracting a proofreader to do a last pass on anything you're submitting.

Happy writing!

Amy's Field Notes: Why Grammar Matters

Despite having a pretty easy name to spell, I still get coffee cups with "Ami" or "Amee" written on them. The jokes about baristas spelling names wrong is as old as time, but it's something people recognize. *Oh, they spelled my name wrong.*

The mistake sticks out like a sore thumb, even though it's probably just a blip in your or the barista's day.

Now, imagine you paid $4,000 for that coffee cup at a high-end, luxury coffee shop buried somewhere in the Swiss Alps. You're expecting it to contain the *most epic mocha ever*. You're smelling the organic cashew milk and the dark chocolate. You're in Switzerland, expecting a cup that will change your life.

But when you get your hella expensive coffee, your name is misspelled on the cup. How would you feel knowing you spent all this money on a fancy experience, and they couldn't even be bothered to spell your name right?

While not all of your errors in copywriting will be as bad as misspelling someone's name (although I've seen *plenty* of experienced copywriters misspell names of clients, companies, and names of the client's own book) it still sticks out. The mistake reads as: "I couldn't be bothered to double-check this."

I was reading a popular freelance writer's book the other day, and came across multiple spelling and grammar errors they had left in the *published book*. I was horrified for them. What better way to ruin your credibility with your readers and potential clients than to make mistakes in something that's supposed to be the epitome of your written work?

When spelling and grammar are done right, they're invisible. It's the mistakes that lose you the trust of your clients.

PART I: GETTING STARTED AS A FREELANCE WRITER

CHAPTER 14:
FROM BEGINNER TO EXPERT: THE FREELANCE FLYWHEEL

On occasion, I take on select freelance writers as coaching clients[8]. I love working one-on-one with writers who want to get a personalized crash course on how to grow their businesses and avoid the mistakes I made in my journey.

I was working with this one coaching client who was having a hard time getting started. She felt overwhelmed with all of the work that it took to get her career off the ground, and as she was searching through jobs, she felt discouraged.

So, I hopped on a call with her to break it down.

Why Getting Started is So Hard

"The reason it's so hard in the beginning is because you don't have momentum yet," I explained on a call with my client. "Nobody knows you're a freelance writer, so how should they know where to find you or how to hire you? Part of the work is educating potential clients on who you are and what you have to offer."

"But I got into freelance writing to write, not to be a full-time marketer!" she said, distraught.

---

[8] Want to learn more about my coaching options? Visit: amysuto.com/six-figure-freelancer

"And you won't be. Marketing is part of the job, sure. Any self-employed person has to learn how to market and sell one's skills. But do you know how much time I spend marketing my skills each week now?"

"How much?"

"Maybe an hour a week. That's it."

"Wow. But how do you get new clients?"

"They find me through search engines, through social media, or through referrals from my past clients or people who know me. But most of my clients are returning clients, and the more clients I work with, the more that come back to me looking to hire me for more work. Do you see how that works?"

"Yeah, but how long will it take me to get there?" she asked.

"Well, how many clients do you have now?"

"None yet."

"Exactly, and that's because you haven't even started yet. But because you have no clients, and no track record, you don't have the momentum of people recommending you, finding your work, or seeing a freelance portfolio or website full of testimonials and past work. You're having to push so hard just to build those things, but once they're built, they start working *for* you. As a new freelancer you have to build assets like a blog that create passive leads and interest in your work as a freelancer so that you don't have to go find new clients—instead, they constantly find you."

"Got it," she said, perking up. "So, this isn't forever?"

"Not in the least," I said with a smile. "But this is the valley of darkness where most people quit. You have to get through this period in order to make it to the other side."

The Freelance Flywheel: How Your Career Works for You

In his book *Good to Great*[9], author Jim Collins breaks down the difference between good and great companies. He coined the term *flywheel* as it relates to companies. A flywheel was a device used in machinery that took a ton of effort to get moving. But once the discs started turning?

---

9   For more book recommendations, visit: amysuto.com/six-fig-ure-freelancer

PART I: GETTING STARTED AS A FREELANCE WRITER

The flywheel was unstoppable, speeding up and sustaining momentum, as if by magic.

When people ask me about how I've built a career as a six-figure freelancer, they're observing a flywheel I've spent years building momentum with. It looks like magic, but it's not.

POSTING YOUR BLOG AND SOCIAL MEDIA ABOUT EXPERTISE TO GAIN CLIENTS

SUBMITTING TO JOBS ON FREELANCE PLATFORMS

RESEARCHING AND COLD-EMAILING COMPANIES

Here's the secret: new freelancers' flywheels look like the above image. They have to expend a ton of energy learning their craft, building their portfolio, and when it comes to finding clients, all of their work is outreach.

You'll notice things change with this second image.

INVITATIONS TO INTERVIEW AND INCOMING WORK ON FREELANCE PLATFORMS

REFERRALS AND INTROS TO NEW CLIENTS FROM PAST (HAPPY!) CLIENTS

PEOPLE FINDING YOU ON SOCIAL MEDIA AND ON YOUR BLOG

RETURNING CLIENTS

New freelancers have to actively sell and market their skills. But once you've gained experience and a reputation for great work, notice how the arrows reverse.

As an expert freelancer or independent artist/creative, you have a lot of incoming work that's been generated by past efforts. Your reputation compounds, your current clients come back to you, and they refer you to others. Your blog posts and Internet presence also generates momentum, and returns your time investment of creating those materials!

When you're a new freelancer, it's hard to even comprehend what being an expert can look or feel like, which is why transparency is critical. As an expert, it's important for me to share a look behind the curtain so you can see how this stuff builds.

What Expert Freelance Writers Have That You Don't

People love talking about passive income. When it comes to freelance writing, the career itself is still "active" income for the most part, but what you can do is make parts of the process more passive. Some freelancers choose to outsource parts of their process like proofreading, editing, or lead generation.

But the momentum of the Freelance Flywheel—when built correctly!—can create passive leads for you forever: no outsourcing required.

So, when you're examining the career of an expert freelancer and wondering, *how on earth is that person making so much?* just know that Rome wasn't built in a day, and neither will your freelancing career. You have to be in this for the long-term. Anyone who promises you a get-rich-quick scheme is likely going to profit off of your greed. Nothing great in life can be accomplished without consistent time and energy, so know there aren't any shortcuts. Instead, apply strategies and build systems: this will optimize your energy and help it compound.

Keep Going

Remember that coaching client I mentioned at the beginning of this chapter? She's killing it. After understanding the concept of the Freelance Flywheel, she booked her first gig—a big win for her that launched her freelance career, and has been working nonstop ever since.

Your first win might be one perspective shift away!

Amy's Field Notes: From Film School Graduation to Now

I was graduating from USC's prestigious film school. I was standing in a hallway, wearing my cap and gown, thinking about the future. All of us were talking about post-graduation, beaming with the excited energy of what was next.

"I hope we'll all make it," I said wistfully, as making it in the film industry was on my mind in those final days of school.

One of my male classmates just grinned and replied: "of course we all will."

His confidence floored me. I knew he came from money, and had industry connections already. But how could he be so sure? Was I missing something?

Fast-forward seven years later: my former classmate is approaching thirty and is still an assistant. And me? Well, I've talked enough here about my journey. Neither of us "made it," but I'm not rolling someone else's calls for them. Instead, I hire other people to help me with my creative projects and get to travel the world thanks to my freelance work.

This isn't to brag: it's to show the difference between investing in turning your own flywheel, or burning your prime years turning someone else's.

If you're always contributing to someone else's momentum, you're never going to have time to build your own compounding returns.

PART 1: GETTING STARTED AS A FREELANCE WRITER

CHAPTER 15:
YOUR POST-PROJECT CHECKLIST

Before you turn in your work, it's *always* important to double-check what you've written to make sure it's truly **good to go**. Nothing's more embarrassing than sending in a draft of something that's riddled with typos or misspellings of your client's name or remnants of your notes to yourself. I know because I've felt the pain of making these mistakes when I was a new freelancer. Nothing screams "sloppy" like glaring errors that take away from the time and energy you put into the rest of the assignment!

Obvious errors are also an immediate red flag to your client. Whether they tell you or not, they're making their decisions on whether or not they're going to recommend you or hire you again based on your work in that moment.

The Post-Job Checklist

Here's the checklist I usually go through when I'm completing an assignment:

- Did I read the instructions correctly? Is there anything the client said in my call with them or in their written instructions that I missed?
- Is everything spelled correctly?
- Are the font sizes and types uniform?
- Did I put a title and version # and date on this document?
- Is everything laid out on the page in a pleasing way? Are there document headings and/or page numbers for documents over three pages

that I can add to make it look even more high-end and professional?
- Did I use the right tense throughout?
- Are all the details accurate and well-researched?
- Re-read the instructions the client sent: did I complete everything?
- Does the writing jump off the page in a compelling way?
- Is there anything I can improve on to make it even 1% better?
- One more time: re-read client instructions. Anything they sent over, they're going to want to see in the final doc, so just re-read them to be sure!
- One last proofreading/grammar check.

Feel free to add your own items to this list (am I sending a funny joke to my client with this email? Is there a pleasing GIF of a cat jumping out of this cake that would go great with this?) but at the end of the day, do whatever you can to hold yourself and your work to the same standard you would hold a freelancer to that you've hired.

Keeping up with ~~The Kardashians~~ Former Clients

Once a job is complete, your client sails off into the ether with your awesome work under their arm, out to change the world with your well-written memoir/copy/blog post on how dubstep is actually aliens just trying to communicate with us. It is :)

But that's not the end: in fact, most of my clients are actually return clients, or referrals from my current set of clients.

By staying on your former clients' radars, you can easily keep up a stable of awesome clients you can work with again and again.

Now *that's* the start of a beautiful friendship.

If you don't already, you might want to consider using a spreadsheet or CRM to track your clients. Every quarter or so, go through that list and send off a "hey, how's it going?" email. Wish them happy holidays, let them know you're thinking of them, and move on. Be casual, be kind, and just offer some good vibes.

What you don't want to do is go after former clients and consistently ask them for more work. You don't want to beg for anything. Let them come to you. It's about staying on their minds, not staying on payroll. Just being on their radar will mean you'll be first on their mind when a new project comes up.

Amy's Field Notes: Peanut Butter Jelly Time? It Depends.

When I was in third grade, my teacher gave us an assignment that seemed super simple: write directions on how to make a peanut butter and jelly sandwich, and write them as if you were explaining it to an alien with no concept of how to make a sandwich. Sounds easy, right? So, my classmates and I wrote down what seemed like a simple writing task.

Next, our teacher whipped out bread, peanut butter, and jelly. Our directions were about to be put to the test! She selected one set of directions at random, and read them aloud as she followed them word-for-word:

"Step one: put the peanut butter on the bread."

Our teacher picked up the entire jar of unopened peanut butter and set it on top of the entire loaf of bread.

"Step two: put the jelly on the bread."

She did the same thing with the unopened jar of jelly.

"Does that look right, class?"

We all laughed, and she reset the sandwich station and picked up another set of directions at random.

"Step one: take two slices of bread and put peanut butter on one of them."

We were off to a better start... but again, our teacher just put the whole jar on top of one slice of bread.

She kept cycling through directions: one set of instructions got more specific with spreading the peanut butter and jelly on both slices of bread, but didn't say what sides should be facing each other (so, our teacher put the dry sides facing each other so the jelly and peanut butter sides faced outwards.)

At the end of the demonstration, she asked us to write the directions again, this time with a new level of specificity. We did, and this time our directions passed the test.

I'm sharing this because your clients will probably give you directions that are crystal clear in their mind—but may lead you astray if they don't specify *exactly how* they want the sandwich made.

Your job as a freelancer is not to just follow instructions as they're received, but to also ask for clarification and confirm that they do want the peanut butter and jelly sides facing outwards (hey, sandwiches can be a deeply personal choice!) before you go ahead and make it that way.

PART 2

THE BUSINESS FUNDAMENTALS OF FREELANCING

PART 2: THE BUSINESS FUNDAMENTALS OF FREELANCING

STORY #2:
A LESSON ON LEVELING UP IN THE WOODS

Dispatches from a Freelance Writer's Life

During my time as an undergrad at USC, I held many different jobs. One of which was an Orientation Advisor, a role where I would help new students navigate their summer orientation so they would be prepared to get the most out of the school year when it started.

As part of my training, myself and all the Orientation Advisors went to this camp in the middle of the woods for some good ol' team bonding. And no, we didn't read any weird Latin chants while performing blood sacrifices while we were there. (That's how the football team spends their retreats.)

One of the activities we did, required us to be blindfolded and attached to a rope in the forest. Our mission? To follow the rope, and find our way out of the obstacle course. And if we needed help, we just had to raise a hand.

So, the blindfolds were put on us, we were attached to the rope with a hook, and we started walking. We ducked under trees, walked gingerly over logs, and headed toward some unknown destination…

…and we walked…

…and we walked…

And around me, I started to hear some giggles. What were people laughing about? I wasn't sure. I was determined to get through the course, but it felt a little endless. I kept walking. And walking. And walking.

And kept hearing more and more giggles and laughter.

Finally, I gave up. I raised my hand, and someone came over and unclipped my hook and took off my blindfold to reveal—

—a perfect circle. We weren't traipsing through the woods on some epic obstacle course: we had been walking through a perfect circle.

The goal of this exercise—the way you "won"—was by raising your hand and asking for help. I was one of the last stubborn ones still walking, unable to ask for help.

At first, I thought the exercise was a little silly, and that the game was rigged. But years later, I realized that during some of the most critical points in my life, I got much further by asking for help when I needed it.

Asking for help can materialize in many different ways. It can be as simple as asking a client to hop on a call to get more information about a project or their company. Or, it can be as complex as needing to hire a proofreader or editor to help you keep the quality of your work high.

When I was diagnosed with rheumatoid arthritis, I had to ask my partner Kyle for help. My disease made it difficult to type—the core part of my job as a freelance writer—and I had to find new ways to automate some of the rote tasks I was doing each day and get help where I needed it. I've also asked for help from the freelancers who have worked with me. I've asked for help redesigning my website, handling my taxes and bookkeeping, and I've asked for help from friends and family when I went through tough times.

This section of the book is here to encourage you to learn the business side of freelancing and then get help where you need it from professionals and other experts. Most freelancers don't think about the "business" side of their work, because most of us are solopreneurs. However, you're doing yourself a disservice by not seeing your work as a business and getting necessary support as you build your brand.

This section is also one of the most powerful: by seeing your work as a business, you can unlock new ways to free up your time, travel the world, and find new and exciting clients.

So don't skip this section: it might just set you free.

PART 2: THE BUSINESS FUNDAMENTALS OF FREELANCING

CHAPTER 16:
"BUSINESS SCHOOL" FOR FREELANCERS

If you're a freelancer, you're also a business owner. If it's just you and you don't have any subcontractors or assistants, you're what's known as a "solopreneur." You do your own thing, sell your services to clients, and maximize profit and minimize loss.

This book isn't financial advice, and that's why I recommend assembling your "Avenger's Team" of experts.

This expert team can include…

- A **lawyer** to handle your contract creation and be there if things go south with a client.
- A **business manager** to handle things like documents related to your business entity and anything else that comes up. This person could also be your accountant and bookkeeper as well.
- An **accountant** to help you with your books and taxes.
- A **freelancer coach or other mentor** to hold you accountable. This could be substituted by just reading books like this one!
- Your **freelancing peers** who you can ask questions about what they're doing with their business and setup.

I credit part of my success to having a trusted team of advisors, mentors, and peers to help steer me in the right direction. Things like tax write-offs can be deeply confusing without having a CPA who is a master of the tax code to help you handle them.

While I'll go over some things you may want to think about for your freelance contract in the next chapter, you should always always always consult a lawyer and have them draw up the paperwork you may use for the rest of your freelance writing career to help protect you in case something goes south.

When it comes to putting yourself through a mini "business school," here are some ways you can teach yourself what you're missing:

- **Read books** about marketing to help you build your website and share your services across social media and blog channels. At the end of this book, you'll find a book list and links for more resources to help you level up your skills as a freelance writer!

- **Learn about the art of negotiation** from experts such as hostage negotiator Chris Voss by watching his Masterclass or reading his book, *Never Split the Difference*[10].

- **Read through IRS tax law** to get familiar with the rules when it comes to tax write-offs for things like business travel (i.e., attending a conference for your freelance field) and other common write-offs so you can work with your CPA effectively during tax season.

- **Learn more about psychology and conflict resolution** so you can work with clients better, even if something goes wrong.

- **Learn about investing**, and decide how you want to build passive income or different streams of income for yourself (more about passive income later in this book!)

- **Get familiar with your state and federal laws** when it comes to freelancing, forming LLCs or whatever entity you are freelancing un-

---

10   For more book recommendations, visit: amysuto.com/six-figure-freelancer

der, and any other details relevant to you and your work.

All of this doesn't have to happen overnight. Just take an hour every week to try and grow your knowledge of the business side of things and ask your team of experts any questions you run into!

The Sixteen Steps to Building a Bulletproof Freelance Business

Here's what I would recommend for the "order of operations" when it comes to setting up your freelance business:
1. Set up an LLC or entity to freelance under. Reach out to both an accountant and a lawyer to get this set up.
2. Open a business bank account for all of your business expenses.
3. Consider professional liability insurance as a freelancer and discuss this with your team of experts.
4. Hire a lawyer to draft the freelancing agreement you will use with clients. If you plan to work with subcontractors or other freelancers, have your lawyer draw up a contract for them as well.
5. Consider getting a PO box or mailbox/street address for your business. This is helpful to keep your home address private while still having an address to list for your business/on contracts/on government documents.
6. Consider getting a separate phone number for your business as well (that you can use with your current phone) so you can reduce spam calls to your personal number and better clock-out on weekends.
7. Create a website for your freelance writing business and list it on Google so people can find you.
8. Talk to your CPA about self-employed tax deductions and the best practices for saving receipts and other record keeping.
9. Keep all your business records in one secure (virtual!) place on your computer or in a Dropbox folder so you always have access to them no matter where you are.
10. Consider getting a business credit card to build credit. Always pay off the balance each month.
11. Do your own bookkeeping or hire a bookkeeper to do that for you.
12. If you have an employee at your freelance business such as a virtual

assistant, you may be able to buy group health insurance plans in certain states. Talk to a health insurance broker who may be able to bundle different insurance plans together for you (i.e., vision/dental/life insurance) depending on your state and your state's marketplace. Otherwise, decide what you're going to do for health insurance, such as purchasing from your state's marketplace as an individual. Look at different options and see what makes sense for your medical spending.
13. If you work with freelancers or employees, talk to your expert team about getting a worker's comp policy.
14. Consider opening a ROTH IRA to save for retirement, but talk to your CPA to see what they recommend for your retirement fund.
15. Consider opening an HSA if you have a high-deductible health plan (HDHP) to both invest your money and use it as needed for qualifying medical expenses. Talk to your CPA about IRS rules for this, and get to know the differences between health insurance plans. Call a health insurance broker if you want to know more.
16. Decide what billing/invoicing and contract management platform you'll use to handle contracts with clients.[11]

When it comes to building a solid foundation for your business, it's worth the time and energy to do it right. A lot of this stuff only has to be done once, so check it off your list and celebrate!

Why Learning About Business Helps You Make More as a Freelance Writer

"But I became a freelance writer just to write!"

Listen, I get it. I recognize that this part of the book might feel akin to "eating your vegetables." But the reason why you eat your vegetables is because it nourishes your body.

Keeping your freelance business healthy will aid you through maximizing tax deductions, reducing risk in case a project does go south, and allowing you to do what you love every day. As you increase your

---

[11] Want to get my top recommendations on the best tools for freelancers? Visit: amysuto.com/six-figure-freelancer

earnings, you can outsource more of the day-to-day business stuff, such as having a bookkeeper do your books, letting your business manager help you with things like billing and other odds and ends, and relying on a lawyer to handle any legal stuff that comes up.

Let's say you *don't* take the time to build the foundation of your freelance business. You don't set up an LLC, you don't create contracts, and you get into legal trouble with a client. They drag you to court, and you could potentially end up being personally liable for whatever damages they're seeking. If you don't have insurance and can't pay whatever the fees are, you might lose personal assets in the process.

I don't say this to scare you—it's rare (but not impossible!) to have a freelance job go this wrong. But it's important to protect yourself in the small chance you do end up doing business with someone who is out to get you. There are some bad apples in the world: don't let them stop you from taking risks and standing up for yourself, but do be sure to take steps to protect yourself so you can move confidently in your work.

A good foundation is like a tree. The best time to plant for some shade was twenty years ago. The second-best time is today.

Amy's Field Notes: You're Only as Good as Your Team

In college, I wrote and produced several hours' worth of scripted content for USC's television station. I ran quite an operation: at one point, I had hundreds of volunteers helping to produce my show about con artists running amuck on a college campus, and students could even earn class credit by working on my crew.

As with any college film project, the episodes of my show varied wildly when it came to quality. We had a rotating list of DPs (Directors of Photography), some of whom knew their way around a camera, some who were more green.

During the episode where our con artists get locked in the radio station and are forced to play a high stakes game of monopoly together, the director opted to do constant 360 rotating shots that worked for a bit—before they became totally dizzying.

This is par for the course when everyone is working for class credit, but when our episodes *did* knock it out of the park—that was all thanks to our crew, as well. A great team could make any challenging shoot day yield high returns.

Our show ended up being nominated for two College Television Emmys, and I traveled with the cast and crew to Miami where we won Best Actor and Best Drama, and I ended up giving an impromptu speech onstage, where I thanked the people who got us there: our team.

You're only as good (or as bad!) as your team, so when hiring teammates to help you in the freelance space, choose wisely, or else you'll end up being the mark during the heist.

PART 2: THE BUSINESS FUNDAMENTALS OF FREELANCING

CHAPTER 17:
CRAFTING YOUR FREELANCE WRITING AGREEMENT

It's a warm summer day in Brooklyn, NY, and as I'm writing this chapter, my freelance writing contract has just saved me from being exploited by one of my clients.

Most of the time, I love my clients. While we might not be skipping down the sidewalk together, I value positive, professional relationships with mutual respect.

In instances like the one I found myself in this afternoon, I still sing the praises of a great freelance contract. You never realize how critical a few pages of a legal document are until you need them the most. In my case, I've found myself in less-than-ideal working conditions, and for some projects, had to delicately disentangle myself from a project gone wrong.

So, my lawyer just tapped me on the shoulder and I have to share a quick disclaimer before we dive into this section: this is not legal advice. It should not be construed as such. You should always consult with a lawyer who knows your unique setup and situation and have them create your contract for you. Internet search engines are not your friend in this situation, especially because the law is complex on purpose. The money you'll spend on a great lawyer is money you'll never regret spending! My lawyer just nodded and disappeared back through the wardrobe. Okay, we're good.

That said, take this chapter as simply my perspective as a freelance writer, and the things I bring up when I talk to my lawyer about my own contracts. Cool? Cool.

Why You Need a Freelancer Contract

Simply put, a contract is a way for you and your client to get on the same page about the project you're about to embark on, and the expectations of your working relationship and how you'll be paid.

A contract is a sign of mutual respect. If your client does not want to sign a contract with you, that's a sign that they do not respect you and your professional work.

Freelancer agreements are also often required by professional liability insurance. Without a contract, it's much harder to enforce payment for your services if your client refuses to pay.

Contracts are also a way to enforce the scope of work. In your freelancing career, you will run across clients that will either try to exploit you, knowingly or unknowingly, if they don't realize the terms of your agreement or forget about how many revisions they agreed you would do.

Contracts get all the details in super clear terms that both you and your client can refer back to during the term of your working relationship together.

What's in a Freelance Contract

Your freelancer agreement (which may be called something like a master services agreement) is the paperwork that spells out the work you will do for a client and what you'll receive in terms of payment.

Your contract will probably include:

- Contract terms
- Statement of work
- Signature page

The contract terms are the meat of your contract, and are what you apply to every single project. Your terms might also include an NDA and contact info for yourself/your company that you freelance under, and your client/client's company.

The Statement of Work (SOW) details specifics to the writing project or engagement you're doing for a particular client, and this often can include things like deadlines, pricing, and more.

PART 2: THE BUSINESS FUNDAMENTALS OF FREELANCING

The signature page is where both you and your client sign.

Things to Think About When Having a Lawyer Create Your Paperwork

When you're creating your paperwork with a lawyer, you're going to want to think about previous projects you've done as a freelancer. What jobs went wrong? What happened? How can you include wording that is clear so that won't happen again in the future? Or, if you're a brand-new freelancer, just keep the following questions in mind as you start to assemble your first contract.

What to think about for your freelance contract:

- How and when do I invoice, and how and when do clients pay me?
- How many rounds of optional revisions do I include in my assignments? Do clients still have to pay me the full amount even if they have no notes and don't need those optional revisions?
- Am I working on a fixed-rate or hourly basis? If both, will my lawyer include language for different types of projects?
- What is my payment schedule?
- How do I get paid? In what currency? When I'm creating my contracts, I like to be specific with this (i.e., $100 USD not just $100), especially as I work with international clients.
- What happens if I cancel the job? If the client does? What are different ways a project can get canceled, and what happens with outstanding payments and ownership of work?
- How is ownership of the material handled?
- What happens if a client doesn't pay an invoice?
- Are there late fees on unpaid invoices?
- How are disputes resolved?
- How can damages be claimed?
- Can I utilize subcontractors like proofreaders to complete my work?

To get even more specific, here are some things you may want to think about for hourly contracts:

- Do I have a limit or ceiling for hourly billing?
- How do I share hour logs with clients?
- Do I bill hours for communication time (i.e., meetings and emails?)
- Do I bill for every hour, half hour, quarter hour? How and when do I round up?
- What is the scope of a project? What am I doing work-wise when I'm billing hours?

And for fixed-rate/flat-fee contracts:

- What happens if the project is canceled mid-milestone?
- Is the initial deposit refundable?
- How many revisions are there? Are these revisions optional (i.e., a client can waive them if they don't need them?)
- At what point is the final draft final?
- How long do clients have to give notes on a first draft? Indefinitely? Two weeks?
- How long is my timeline as the writer for delivering each draft?

A great lawyer should walk you through some of this, but remember that you know your business best, so take initiative on making sure the common things that go wrong are covered for you.

Your Statement of Work

When I'm putting together a contract, I pay particular attention to the statement of work. When I send a quote to a client for a fixed-rate project, I get super specific on the details. My statement of work includes the project name, the upper word count maximum, the number of optional revisions, and any other details that describe what I'm writing for my client and what the final deliverable should look like. For hourly projects, I describe the project and the writing work I will be doing for that project, and include communication such as email and calls in my statement of work.

Everyone's contract is personal, which is why I stay away from prescribing what you should do in this chapter or sharing my own contract terms or exact statement of work. Your business, types of assignments, and local laws will look different than mine, which is why you need a professional to get this key document just right. Your contract is not a fixed thing: it is an organism, a co-worker, and it will grow and become more formidable over time. But you really don't know what you need until you need it. So, get out there, and when something spooks you, look at your contract and figure out what to add to keep the boogeyman at bay in your business.

Contracts as an Investment in Your Future

Whew, okay, that might have felt like a lot. But trust me, once you have your rock-solid agreement that you've crafted with the help of a licensed lawyer in your state, you're golden! Keep that lawyer's info on file for any projects that might go south, and now you can move on to more fun parts of the process.

While you have to handle the "business" side of your freelancing business yourself, I always recommend leaning on professionals like lawyers, business managers, and accountants. The urge to DIY a contract is strong, but please don't. Investing in professionals to help you get set up is worth every penny.

Remember: it's better to invest now to protect yourself rather than learn the hard way down the line.

In the next part of this book, we'll go over how to land higher-paying clients so you can continue to see an increase in your income and lead a profitable life as a freelancer.

Amy's Field Notes: The Power of a Great Contract

It doesn't matter how many times I put into writing my arrangement with a client, or if I discuss with them the details of the work I'm doing with them on a call, there will always be one or two clients every few months who don't read the terms of our engagement and somehow think we have unlimited revisions or something crazy like that.

I have to pull up our contract and reference it, saying something along the lines of, "well, if you read in the statement of work, you'll see we have a maximum of two revisions, but if you'd like me to work hourly for the rest of the contract to finish those out, I'd be happy to."

This happened twice during the writing of this book. Both times, the clients confessed they hadn't read the contract, and had no idea what it said. I was floored, but stayed professional.

People don't read. It's a truth that hurts as a professional writer, and it's why your contract is so important. It's an enforcer of your policies and, y'know, the law—and keeps you safe when a client is trying to wiggle out of a payment or change the terms halfway through a contract.

PART 2: THE BUSINESS FUNDAMENTALS OF FREELANCING

CHAPTER 18:
THE ART OF NEGOTIATION

When you hear the word "negotiation," do you imagine a bunch of people in suits in a boardroom arguing over money? Yeah, I did too when I started.

These days, negotiation to me looks like a series of emails:

Me: It was great meeting with you today about your metaverse project set in the meowverse where Ancient Egyptian cats have come back to rule the world! Based on what you want for this project, here's my proposal with details on how I can help and my timeline. The cost for this would be $5,000.

Client: Any way you could work for a percentage of the project revenue?

Me: No, I only work for my rate. If you want me to remove a rewrite, I could do it for $4,000. Or, I could bundle with other deliverables and give you a 10% discount: that package would be $10,000 not including the discount.

Client: Can you do the large package, but expedite the process? We need all of those deliverables ASAP.
Me: Sure, I can shave three business days off my package for a rush fee of $3,000.

Client: Any way we could do the $10k package with a rush fee for $8k?

Me: Unfortunately not. I would want to make sure I have enough time to do a great job for you and your feline friends on this project, so I can't work below the quoted $10k with the rush fee of $3k. But as I mentioned, I can give you a 10% discount off of that final quote.
Client: Sounds good, let's move forward with that quote so we can honor the legacy of these Ancient Egyptian Cats.

As a freelancer, what you just read looks like setting boundaries, carving out the scope of the project, and offering different packages, discounts, and bundles based on what your client wants and what is worth your time. In other words? A negotiation.

I prefer to discuss money stuff over email, but in the rare exception that I negotiate a deal on a call, I'll follow-up with an email afterward to make sure we get any decisions in writing. Emotions can affect memory, but email is forever (so keep good backups!)

The Basics of Negotiation for Freelance Writers

As I mentioned in earlier sections of this book, I recommend reading Chris Voss' book *Never Split the Difference*[12] or watch his Masterclass course on how to negotiate. He breaks down essentials of human nature and psychology that are important to understand. Even though freelancing isn't intense dealmaking, being able to negotiate with clients is a skill that will pay off every time you begin a new project.

After you hop off a discovery call with a potential client, you'll probably send them a **project proposal** that details the services you can provide based on what their needs are and how you can help. This proposal should include pricing, timeline, billing instructions, and more.

---

12   For more book recommendations, visit: amysuto.com/six-figure-freelancer

Next, the client will either:

a) Accept your proposal and the project will begin
b) Counter your proposal with a different rate, pay structure, or set of deliverables
c) Reject your proposal or ghost you

When option B happens, the negotiation takes place.

How to Give Your Clients More Value

When I'm in a negotiation, I'll occasionally add some complimentary bonuses to my fixed-rate projects, such as a complimentary SEO strategy session, or a complimentary handout on best practices for the client's project.

Your goal as a freelancer should be to make sure your potential clients feel like you're giving them extraordinary value. This begins with the quality of your work, but it can also help to be generous with other resources or things that your clients might find useful.

Any "freebies" should be clearly defined in your contract (i.e., "one optional and complimentary up-to-fifty-minute strategy session conducted remotely via video or phone call") so that both you and your client understand the scope of these complimentary bonuses.

You can also give a "new client discount" to encourage them to take a chance on you. Or, you could offer a "free project proposal" where you outline how you're going to tackle a project.

It's up to you how you want to structure these add-ons or other ways to give your client peace of mind knowing they've spent their money wisely. At the end of the day, delivering reliable, high-quality work is the core of what creates value for your clients: any additions are simply marketing tools and ways to persuade a client who's on the fence about your rate or hiring you.

The Most Important Rule in ~~Dating~~ Negotiating: Don't Be Desperate

Freelancing is a bit like dating: you can't be desperate. You have to be secure and confident in yourself and your abilities before you enter the ring: otherwise, you'll find yourself ending up in a compromised position and taking a royalty deal from *Shark Tank's* Mr. Wonderful in perpetuity.

This is why future chapters of this book will go over mindset and ways to ride out the emotional rollercoaster of the feast-or-famine life that freelancing can feel like, and how to find calm even in those early, uncertain days of being a freelance writer.

Understanding the economic concept of opportunity cost will help you walk away from projects that aren't going to pay enough or be a good fit for you. The concept of **opportunity cost** states that the cost of your decision is the missed opportunities you could have pursued in place of what you chose. For example, if I choose to stay inside on a sunny day, the cost of my decision is the opportunity to catch some rays and vitamin D.

The cost of taking on a project that you're not excited about may be higher than you think. When your energy is zapped from working with a client who doesn't value you, it's much harder to go out and find the projects and clients who *do* value your time.

When to Walk Away

Want to know what might actually win you a project? Standing your ground on your rate and being willing to walk away if a potential client can't meet you there.

I can't tell you how many projects have accepted my quote even after they said they were unable to pay that much. Remember, your clients are negotiating just as much as you are. If they can't meet you where you're at, it's often better to stand your ground. It will reinforce the perspective in their mind that you're worth the rate you're quoting—and I've had clients who have saved up to hire me and came back around, sometimes two years after our initial meeting!

If you're always chasing your shadow—or clients—then they will never pursue you. The goal as a freelancer is to become a high-end service for your clients. While in some cases I've given out slight discounts on larger packages, it's important to not overuse these tactics. Don't give out continuous discounts or bend to your clients too often, as it won't create the kind of dynamic you want. Trust me.

How much you want to get into the weeds of negotiating your rate is up to you. If you've been working to hone your skills and your knowledge, you have a valuable asset that people will pay well for.

In my mind, it's better to just find better clients than to work with those who can't (or choose not to) afford your rate.

Amy's Field Notes: The Top 1% of Freelancers Work for the Top 1% of Clients

Before I hop on calls with clients these days, I have to check and see if my rates are aligned with their budget, which helps me protect my time as well as my potential client's time.

Today, I did just that, and the client fired back: "I don't like discussing money before meeting on a business engagement."
Which is odd, because usually business engagements require an agreement on price before they move forward. You wouldn't hire an accountant without confirming their rates, why would you try and hire a freelancer without understanding their basic price range?

As someone who has hired freelancers in the past, I've loved getting price clarity before hopping on calls and moving the ball forward. I like to understand their hourly rate, any package pricing, and get to know them and their work. I expect that same courtesy from the clients who want to hire me.

The top freelancers want to work with the top clients, so those who wish to attract and retain top talent will need to show that they're a good client to work with from the start. And what better way than respecting your boundaries and the value of your time.

PART 3

HOW TO LAND BETTER, HIGHER-PAYING CLIENTS

PART 3: HOW TO LAND BETTER, HIGHER-PAYING CLIENTS

STORY #3:
HOLLYWOOD SIGN VIEWS FROM A PARKING LOT APARTMENT

Dispatches from a Freelance Writer's Life

Early in my career as a writer, I lived over a parking lot with a view of the Hollywood sign. I was "moving up in the world" in some ways: it was my first one-bedroom apartment I didn't have to share with a roommate, and my tiny balcony over the parking lot was sunny and key outdoor space in a crowded city. The view of the Hollywood sign also was an intoxicating symbol, and back then, I felt how the industry had a chokehold over me even as I was starting to move on to greener pastures.

At this point, I had already written an episode of TV in my dream genre (spy thriller, of course), and I thought my next job was already in the bag. But when the next job offer did come, it wasn't what I wanted. I realized that my skills were not being valued in Hollywood, whereas my freelance clients were paying me thousands of dollars a month to pen their life stories.

So, when another job offer came in that was also a demotion—yet still a job most in Hollywood would clamor for—I turned it down and booked a flight to Paris. I hired a friend of mine to become my proofreader and editor as I was starting to get inundated with freelance work, and I began thinking beyond the Hollywood sign.

For the longest time, scarcity and traditional ways of thinking held me back. *Who am I to turn down a job on a cool show? Freelance writing can't possibly be more fulfilling than Hollywood. People don't dream of becoming freelance writers, this life isn't as fun.*

In Hollywood, I was represented by managers, had earned a TV writing credit, and had just finished a new pilot and sizzle reel I had filmed in the desert. I was poised for success. Right?

In reality, Hollywood was a hamster wheel with declining jobs, fewer episode orders, and an increase in nepotism due to the TV bubble bursting. In my freelance writing life, however, I was able to write from Berlin and spend a week exploring the city and working on my own creative projects on the side. I went on my first-ever business trip, where I was flown out to meet with a book client who I was doing ghostwriting work for.

My freelance writing unlocked travel, a bug I couldn't shake off. I could now work remotely from NYC, Washington DC, Paris, Berlin—anywhere I wanted to go, the city was mine for the taking. I could do work by day, and end up at a wine and cheese tasting in a Paris cavern at night.

Now *that* was something I couldn't have dreamed of—and wouldn't have been possible—from a writer's room in Los Angeles. Not like this.

It took a long time after that point for me to fully begin to shake the scarcity mindset I had spent years developing. I had to silence the echoes of *nobody will pay me this much money to write. There's no way my skill is that valuable. I can't make a great living from this, not really.*

The way to find success as a freelancer is to work hard, work smart, and know that if you build your career with strategy and focus, you deserve every raise you give yourself. There is no scarcity, because people will pay top dollar for talent and reliability. At the time, I didn't realize how valuable clients and companies found those skills—and I had both.

I never want to paint the time between scarcity and success as easy: breaking these bad habits, creating high-level skillsets for yourself, and learning how to negotiate takes time and energy. Turning down client projects that aren't a right fit for you can hit much harder if your bank account is running low. Burnout is inevitable if you don't set boundaries and a hard schedule for yourself right out of the gate.

It took me a long time to go from tiny studio apartment to tiny one-bedroom overlooking a parking lot with a barely-there view of the Hollywood sign. It took me even longer to go to full-time traveler making six-figures and taking time off when it suits me.

As of the writing of this book, I've been freelancing for about seven years: three years part-time, four years full-time. I still deal with the creeping fear of scarcity, that everything I build will go to zero. But then I remind myself that's not true, and see the facts in front of me. The years of living in fight-or-flight will still take years to reverse.

Even when I went full-time as a freelancer four years ago, I couldn't fight the scarcity mindset and ended up working myself to a place of burnout so severe that it triggered an autoimmune disease. I've had to remake every part of my lifestyle since then, and prioritize taking care of myself and enforcing a positive mindset.

Building a successful six-figure freelance life is a complex enterprise that requires a solid foundation of a positive mindset, problem-solving, and *kind* self-encouragement. It asks for an alchemy of hard numbers and soft feelings. You are a business, but you also are a human being. You have to divide those parts of yourself during your workdays and weekends so that both parts of you can feel taken care of as a whole person.

Freelancing isn't easy: it goes against every piece of programming you learned subconsciously in school. It goes against the ease of societal expectations and can be hard to explain to friends and family who have never existed outside the structure of a 9-to-5 job.

The real question is this: what are you going to prioritize? If the answer is travel, freedom, and the ability to decide when and where you work, I'm glad you've found this book. Your abundance is right around the corner—and you don't need a Hollywood sign to light the way to your true happiness.

PART 3: HOW TO LAND BETTER, HIGHER-PAYING CLIENTS

CHAPTER 19:
WHERE ARE ALL THE HIGH-PAYING CLIENTS?

I get this question—or a variation of this question—all the time. When people find out that I'm making $5,000 as a project *minimum* with my packages ranging up to $35,000, they all want to understand, "where are your clients coming from?! The moon?"

No. Here on regular ol' planet earth. I'll take a second here to tell you a quick story about my dating life, which is actually relevant to the advice I'm about to give you.

Freelancing vs. Dating

When I was dating in my early twenties, I had friends who would tell me their horror stories of the people they were going on dates with. They would get ghosted, end up with men (or women!) who would make them pay for everything, or feel like every interaction was superficial and transactional. According to the people around me, the dating pool in Los Angeles was absolute trash, chivalry was dead, and true human connection was out of style.

When it came time to share my dating stories, I had a very different experience. I had men plan surprise dates for me all around the city from rooftops in Downtown to secret music shows. When I started dating women, I shared some of my experiences in an article published by *The Los Angeles Times* about the magic of dating women I met at my pole dancing studio, and sharing a glimpse into the fun and elaborate dates we'd get up to.

With a few exceptions, my dating history has been filled with fun nights out, lovely people, and deep intimacy and connection. My current partner Kyle takes care of me when I'm sick, makes me laugh when I'm sad, and travels the world with me. I couldn't ask for a better partner, and he inspires me to be a better person on a daily basis.

When my friends ask me where I found all of these people to go on extraordinary dates with in the past—or even how I met my current partner—my answer is that we're all fishing from the same pool, just with different poles.

In college, I decided to embark on one hundred Tinder dates before I started dating my boyfriend at the time whom I worked with. I only ended up going on twenty-seven dates or so, but each of those dates was fun and interesting, despite everyone's claim that Tinder was a hookup app and a toxic wasteland for real conversations.

The *way* I approached all my dates was a huge factor in all of my positive experiences: I was picky about who I selected, and had a criteria in mind before I started swiping. There were immediate red flags that would disqualify a potential date, and those would override all other factors.

The true red flag was if I realized I wasn't vibing with someone—or if I felt they weren't vibing with me in the same way—then I would quickly part ways and move on. I never wanted to waste their time or mine if things felt like they weren't fun and reciprocal.

Funny enough, I think this dating strategy actually helped me get further faster in the world of freelancing.

Here's why:

- **First impressions matter**, so understand how to lean into your good qualities and experience on a first discovery call with a potential client.
- **Learning to see red flags** and turning down clients that aren't right for you will lead you to finding better clients, faster.
- **Understanding what mutual respect looks and feels like** in a client/freelancer relationship will help you cultivate a healthier, happier work life.

Even if you don't consider yourself "good at dating," you can still find those "soulmate clients" in the world of freelancing. Those projects that make you fall in love with writing, all over again? They're out there, waiting. They just require some legwork and good people skills to get to! It's just up to you if you're going to swipe left or right when the opportunity comes.

Where to Find Great Clients

This is the number one question I get all the time. So, let's talk about where new freelancers can find new clients:

- **Freelance platforms:** There are so many amazing freelance platforms and matching websites, with new options popping up every day. As I've mentioned earlier in this book, I recommend you get started here.[13] Clients on freelance platforms often hire within a few days, so speed and constantly applying for jobs is key here.

- **Cold emails:** To be totally honest, I didn't do this at all when I started as a freelancer. I just went all-in on freelance platforms and that did the trick. But if you're not finding traction on freelance platforms, you should pivot to cold emailing clients. This process can be time-consuming: you'll need to research clients you want to work with, dig up their emails, and reach out to the people you're interested in working for. Your cold emails should be personalized (at least a little bit!) so people don't think you're just spamming them. Cold emails are a very active process, but if you don't have enough clients, you'll need to make time for this.

- **In-person at conferences:** Where do your clients hang out or go to learn about industry trends? Conferences and other events in your niche are a great way to meet potential clients, and this is another relatively newer way I've found clients. I've also become a speaker at conferences hosted in cities like NYC and London, which is another great way for me to share my services and knowledge and meet po-

---

13   For more tips on how to get started on freelance platforms, visit: amy-suto.com/six-figure-freelancer

tential clients who can get a better sense of what I can do for them.

- **Online groups and message boards:** Where do your clients hang out online? Join any groups and message boards related to your niche. Just be aware that this is more of a "long game" play as most of these message boards are "no solicitation" so you can't just go sell your services: you need to provide value.

All of these methods require you, the freelancer, to reach out and pitch your services. You can outsource this to someone who specializes in lead generation or to a virtual assistant, but that's not something you'll probably be able to do right when you get started.

If you want to earn more and work less, however, you need to find a more passive way for your clients to find you.

How to Help Great Clients Find You

When I went from finding clients to creating content to help them find me, I finally found the tipping point in my career as a freelancer and the deluge of work hasn't stopped since. So here are my favorite ways to help great clients find you:

- **Write blog posts covering topics they want to learn from you**... and what they can hire you to do for them. Learning search engine optimization (SEO) is a gift that keeps on giving, as once you write one blog post, it's out there forever for people to find. The more you write on your blog, the more traffic comes to your website, and the more people who can find you... you get the idea :)

- **Create social media posts** about topics your ideal audience wants to learn from you. This is another great way to show your expertise (and share that you're available to be hired by them!)

- **Write a book about your niche.** This is a great way to prove that you can write a great book (which will get you work ghostwriting books!) and help you codify your process.

- **Get listed in directories.** Every time I go to a conference, I get listed in their directory as a freelance writer—especially if I'm a speaker. I've gotten lots of leads from conference organizers, so this is another good option.

- **Do great work for your current clients.** I've gotten a good percentage of my clients from referrals! You can also offer current clients a referral bonus for recommending you to other people who may need your services.

There are so many ways you can get active and passive leads, so get creative and dig in deeper! Understand exactly what types of clients you want to work with and go to the source. This takes hard work and persistence, so don't give up.

Go After Higher Paying Jobs, Not a High Volume of Low Paying Jobs

I've touched on this before, but I'll mention it again here as it's critical. When you're pitching clients on your services, you're going to get people who want to try and get your skills at a discount. Or, you may be scrolling through freelance platforms and see that there appears to be a lot of low-paying jobs.

Remember, your worth is not dictated by those numbers. Stand confident in your rates: when you're reaching out to potential clients, you're offering them an incredible opportunity to work with you! If they value that, they'll pay for it. If not, they won't—and that's totally fine.

Going back to the rules of dating, don't be desperate and take people at their word. That's not saying you can't shoot your shot when you lock eyes with someone across the metaphorical bar: even if they seem like a $30/hour job there's no harm in talking with them and sharing your sparkling personality to see if they'll come up to your rates.

That's how you win at freelance platforms and at freelancing in general. You're the hot girl at the bar, and you have to embody that spirit (because we *all* are the hot girl at the bar—we just need to own that!)

Your confidence will inspire others to take a chance on you.

Wait, So There's No More Magic to It?

Great clients are like hearing a great song on the radio. When you find someone you love working with and who loves working with you, it's all harmony from there. But that's the thing: you still found your new favorite song on the radio, or on a streaming platform, or from a well that everyone else has access to.

Sure, you might find a super niche song that you love at a vinyl record store or from a friend's recommendation. Maybe you're at an indie music dance party and the vibe just hits right.

Opportunities are all around you: some require work, some are simply attracted to you.

So put in the legwork to become magnetic, create daily habits that help you reach out to people you want to work for, and let the opportunities flow in.

Amy's Field Notes: Ask for What You Want

One of the biggest days in my freelancing career was when I landed a $22,000 project at the same time as I landed a $15,000 project. Up until that moment, the biggest project I had ever landed was a $15,000 project, so this day was a huge level up for me.

I like to mention this day not to brag, but because I got both of these projects from a popular freelance platform, and anyone else could have reached out to these projects like I did. However, the budgets that were listed for these projects were *waaaay* below what I was comfortable working for.

So, for one project I hopped on a call with the founder and pitched him my skills, my rate, and what I could do for him. I landed the project.

The same day, I was messaging back and forth with another team that wanted to get a quote on some services. I recommended deliverables I offer for teams like them, and gave them a quote. They hired me also.

For both projects, I was confident and sold my services knowing what I could bring to the table. Sure, my past experience helped, but the point here is that I'm not fishing from a separate, special pond. I don't have VIP access to a different area of the club than you. I grew my portfolio, rates, and experience from the ground up over time, and I'm hoping that this book can help you avoid the same mistakes I did—and I hope my wins inspire you to go after the magic I've found working with amazing projects and teams all over the world.

At the end of the day, there's just one not-so-secret tip for how to be a successful freelancer, regardless of how you acquire clients: ask for what you want to be paid, and provide exceptional value in return. I'm doing the easy part of giving you advice, it's up to you to tailor it to your unique situation and niche.

Rinse, repeat, and enjoy an awesome career.

PART 3: HOW TO LAND BETTER, HIGHER-PAYING CLIENTS

CHAPTER 20:
FROM DAY JOB TO FULL-TIME FREELANCE WRITER

So, you've mastered the basics of freelancing, you've done great work for some early clients, and now it's time to quit your full-time job and focus solely on your career as a freelancer.

First, take this moment to celebrate! You're breathing rarified air: most people get stuck in the purgatory between where they are and where they want to be. You're on the precipice, and it's time to jump!

Before You Quit Your Day Job

Before you make any decisions, I always recommend connecting with your CPA (or, if you don't have an accountant, finding one!) and going over your finances. Are you good to make the leap, or do you need to clear some debt first? You don't need to be 1,000% financially in the clear, but you do need to be in a place where you have some runway to get up and running.

Consider larger economic conditions as well. While these won't completely crush your burgeoning freelancing business, it's good to get a sense of what kind of pressures your ideal clients might be facing. I've been able to stay booked and busy even during market slumps and slower summers, but it does require more hustle to find and maintain clients in these climates.

Remember, there is no stability in any type of career: if you're a full-time employee, you could be laid off. If you're a freelancer, clients could run dry. However, from my experience, I've found that spreading that risk across multiple clients and projects is a lot "safer" than being an employee with a single employer.

There's no perfect time to take the leap. Once you've got a small safety net and enough wind beneath your sails, it's time to go for it.

What to Tell Friends and Family

I'm lucky that both my parents were self-employed, so they "got it" when I became a full-time freelancer. I'm also a creative, so stability is not something the people in my life were pressuring me to go and find.

However, I know that might not be the case for you. There might be well-meaning friends and family members who are worried about you because they're projecting their own insecurities. It's important to know the context of the person who is giving the advice, because their experience affects what they recommend to you. They probably don't understand what the freelance market looks like these days, and how it's changed over the years and been supercharged by technology and remote work tools.

Here's what I recommend sharing with them:

> The freelance platform Upwork conducts a ton of research on the state of freelancing, and their data shows that "60% of freelancers who left a full-time job to become freelancers make more money than they did in their previous jobs"[14] and a CNBC article stated that "[f]reelancers working in web/mobile development, marketing, legal, accounting, and other skilled services earn an even higher $28/hour average wage. At $28/hour, these freelancers are making more than 70% of all workers in the United States."[15]

---

14   https://www.upwork.com/press/releases/freelancers-union-and-upwork-release-new-study-revealing-insights-into-the-almost-54-million-people-freelancing-in-america

15   https://www.cnbc.com/2019/10/03/skilled-freelancers-earn-more-per-hour-than-70percent-of-workers-in-us.html

PART 3: HOW TO LAND BETTER, HIGHER-PAYING CLIENTS

Basically? The statistics are in your favor. I've experienced this momentum firsthand: I went from earning $90/hour to $350/hour after going full-time freelance. You can hit your goals with time and consistent effort!

Even if you don't accelerate as quickly as I did, you're set to make a lot more money than you probably are making now on a good timeline.

Use this data and any other anecdotal evidence you have to help reassure friends and family, but know that any disapproval you might get from them often stems from an irrational place of care and worry for you.

Just take a breath and keep going.

What to Do After You Quit Your Day Job

When you quit a full-time job and walk out of your office or log off your work email for the last time, you will probably feel a mix of emotions.

Did I make the right choice?

Am I crazy to walk away from my job?

I'm freeeeeeeeeeeeeee!

Hang on to the last one and let the other worries go the best you can. It's time to buckle down and focus!

Here's what I recommend you do immediately after quitting your day job (some you'll see are from my checklist earlier):

1. **Celebrate!** Take a few days off, celebrate with friends or family, or throw a party. Enjoy your next step in life's great adventure!

2. **Re-evaluate your personal and business budget.** Now that you're reliant on your freelance income, get clear on your runway, your personal and freelance business budgets, and your target income.

3. **Meet with a CPA to set up your business entity.** You're going to need an entity at some point to help you organize business expenses and shield you in case of any potential legal issues, so if you don't already have one, talk to your CPA and/or a lawyer about setting one up. I recommend you find an expert to help you rather than relying on an online service to do this for you.

4. **Handle your health insurance and retirement account needs.** Your CPA can also help with this, but make sure you've got your self-employment benefits figured out now that you don't have an employer handling these.

5. **Spread the word!** Tell everyone you're freelancing full-time now! Ask friends and co-workers to share your services with people who might be interested, and ask current clients for testimonials you can put on your website and let them know you have more availability if they have additional work. It's time to grow!

6. **Get your new workspace set up.** Spend some time getting your new work-from-home setup feeling cozy, or simply refresh your existing setup if you were already working remotely. Maybe buy some fresh flowers or light a candle: find ways to make your new job feel like home! Remember, you don't need a fancy home office to be a freelancer. Your workspace could be the dining room table, a quiet nook in your home, a co-working space, or even on a beach in a foreign country. Wherever you are, create a space that feels welcoming!

7. **Create new daily rituals and routines.** Feel free to refer back to my tips on maker/manager schedules, but don't be afraid to add some spice. Maybe you have a noon dance party? Maybe you make an epic brunch every Friday morning for you and your family? Or, maybe a trip to a museum is in the cards for an afternoon, or a mid-week stroll? You make your own schedule, now, so design it the way that works best for you!

Freelancing can get lonely sometimes, so make sure you're also taking time to cultivate community in different aspects of your life. This can be as simple as taking an afternoon yoga class or joining a book club.

You can also attend conferences for your industry as a freelance writer, which is a great way to meet potential clients and go on a tax-deductible trip. (For more on business tax deductions and travel I recommend that—you guessed it!—you talk to your accountant.)

PART 3: HOW TO LAND BETTER, HIGHER-PAYING CLIENTS

Why More Time = More Momentum

When you quit your day job, you have more time to dedicate to your freelancing career, which increases your chances of success.

It was when I adjusted my focus from a lamp (scattered) to a laser (sharp) that I saw huge jumps in my income and the viability of my freelance career. I learned how to implement value-based pricing, I got educated on my niche, and I kicked my systems into gear so I could spend less time on admin work and client onboarding.

So, if you're not seeing your freelancing ramp up to where you want to be as a part-time freelancer, the answer may be to gather your courage and make the leap.

And then, once you do, it's time to hone your systems so you can make your work more efficient. Now, it's time to earn more while working less—and still providing insane amounts of value to your clients, who will come back and re-book you time and time again.

Amy's Field Notes: Hammer Museum Writing Vibes

It was a Wednesday in Los Angeles, so I decided to do some work at the Hammer Museum. I drove from my Mid-City apartment down Wilshire, past all of the busy Hollywood people speeding back from their lunch breaks.

Instead, I leisurely made my way to the west side, where I posted up at the Hammer Museum's courtyard for a new perspective on the writing I was doing that day. I brought my favorite leather-bound notebook, bought myself a coffee from the cafe, and people watched and doodled in my notebook. The sun dripped from in-between the trees, and a soft breeze kept me company.

This is heaven, I thought, remembering the artificial fluorescent light that used to be my only warmth in cold offices. Now, I was surrounded by art and sunlight, and wasn't going to be trapped inside all day.

After I wrapped up my work for the day, I went to my favorite yoga studio to take a class, and then headed to an art exhibit I had been hired to write about.

In those early days of freelancing, I was still filled with uncertainty. I wasn't sure if I was being silly by leaning so hard in freelancing, but I couldn't shake the feeling that life was just *better* without a 45-minute morning commute in traffic and mornings spent eating breakfast to-go while I rushed through morning emails at the office.

Despite the advantages of freelancing, you may still feel a deep sense of anxiety as you're getting started. This is normal, too. You may even feel like you're unable to be grateful for your new flexible schedule and luxuries like staying at home in your PJs while the rest of the world is braving rush hour.

This is okay: your feelings are valid. Spend time journaling as you work through the programming that kept you in the hamster wheel. You're not missing anything by stepping out of the infinite loop.

PART 3: HOW TO LAND BETTER, HIGHER-PAYING CLIENTS

CHAPTER 21:
AUTOMATING YOUR CLIENT WORKFLOW

"You do not rise to the level of your goals. You fall to the level of your systems."

That quote is from one of my favorite books, *Atomic Habits* written by James Clear[16]. I stumbled across this book at a pivotal moment in my freelancing career, and it completely changed the way I approached my life and my work. Instead of setting ambitious goals, I ditched goals completely and created vision boards and robust systems.

The combination of positive visualizations and bulletproof systems helped to get me where I am today: financially free and traveling the world.

However, I'd be lying if I said that getting here was easy. It took a lot of trial and error to build the automations and systems I have in place now, so don't get frustrated if it takes you some time to figure out what you need in your life.

So, if you're at a place in your freelancing career where you want to work less while earning more, it's time to make your systems more efficient.

Step One: Audit Your Daily Workflow

Let's get started by getting a better sense of what you do every day. Create a list of your daily tasks that happen more than once. This could be invoicing a client, following up on an invoice, creating a client contract,

---

16 For more book recommendations, visit: amysuto.com/six-figure-freelancer

or adding someone to your email newsletter list.

For the next seven days, add anything you do more than once to your list. Even a trivial task that's taking you ten minutes per day to complete is still nearly an hour lost per workweek! What could you do with that hour if you were able to give it back to yourself? Take a nap? Go on a hike? Take a nap in the middle of your hike? The possibilities are endless.

After you've created your list, estimate how long that task took you TOTAL for the entire week of completing it.

Step Two: Outsource or Automate

Okay, you have your list. I'll create a sample list to show you what mine looked like.

Tasks I do more than once each week:

1. Send and follow-up on invoices - 30 minutes
2. Send and follow-up on contracts - 30 minutes
3. Send clients/potential clients times to meet - 30 minutes
4. Send clients/potential clients calendar invites and confirm meetings - 30 minutes
5. Follow-up with potential clients post-meeting - 2 hours
6. Do research for an assignment - 4 hours
7. Proofread an assignment before turning in - 3 hours
8. Manage my schedule for the week - 30 minutes
9. Post blog posts to various channels - 30 minutes
10. Send proposals and cold emails - 15 hours

That list might resemble what you're working with. Or, you might have more unique problems you're trying to solve. Either way, let's get into the weeds together so we can give you back more of your time!

Let's begin by tackling the tasks that are taking up the most of your precious time. For me, that was sending proposals and cold emails.

This was taking me a crazy *15 hours per week* as a new freelancer. This isn't uncommon when you're getting started, but there had to be a better way.

As part of this task, I was submitting unique proposals on freelance

PART 3: HOW TO LAND BETTER, HIGHER-PAYING CLIENTS

platforms to jobs I was applying for, and finding a select number of companies I was reaching out to for freelance work. I had to track down email addresses, write cold emails, and ship them off every week. I was working through a spreadsheet of wish list clients, and I would take hours to go through it each week, trying to personalize every single one.

It might be daunting to look at a task like this. You might even throw up your hands and say, *it's just part of the job*!

But it's not. Not really. Let's get some help with this, okay?

For this task, ask yourself: can I **automate** or **outsource** this task? For my example in particular, I decided to do both.

The first thing I did early in my career was to hire a friend as a virtual assistant for a few hours per week. I wasn't paying her a ton—just $20/hour—but she saved me hours of work. To begin, I just had her help with small tasks. She had time in her schedule and wanted a part-time gig, so it worked out perfectly. (More on hiring a virtual assistant in the next chapter!)

Eventually, I decided to have my virtual assistant help me with submitting proposals on freelance platforms. I generated my template cover letters, told her which jobs I wanted to be put up for, and had her take over that work. I gave her feedback as she went, giving her pointers and feedback to help her be more accurate. It worked: I no longer had to be sending out all those proposals on freelance platforms.

For the second part of the task, I created a spreadsheet with all of the potential clients I wanted to work with. From there, I tracked down emails for marketing execs and founders. Then, with the help of my partner Kyle, we worked together to create an email campaign using some automation tools. A quick Internet search will bring up the tools that you can use to do this! These tools automatically sent emails out to everyone on my list—and personalized each email based on the spreadsheet information!—as soon as a new entry was added.

With a combination of automation and outsourcing, I regained those fifteen hours per week. I incurred a new weekly cost of around $200 per week for my virtual assistant and the automation software, but at the time, I had already scaled up past $100/hour, so the jobs I was booking were easily covering this added cost after I billed more than two hours.

By giving myself those hours back, I had more incoming work, more jobs, more revenue, and more free time.

That's the power of automations and outsourcing.

But don't stop there: keep going through your list and see what else you can automate or outsource.

> ✷ **Quick Tip: Stay Up-to-Date with Technology**
>
> Even if you can't automate something now, you might be able to automate it in the future. AI technology is rapidly evolving, leaving a lot of tools in the dust. Every year, do an audit of the tools you're using and see what next-gen technology is available to make your workflow smarter and faster.

Don't Worry: AI Can't Replace Freelance Writers

As of the writing of this book, artificial intelligence has yet to become fully sentient and replace writers. Even the latest language models at best imitate human writing, and at worst are riddled with inaccuracies and cookie-cutter copy.

I wanted to include this section in the book to allay your fears that AI will replace writers, because at the end of the day, **good writing is good thinking**. AI may be able to generate a thousand different catchphrases, but great writers and marketers will still need to curate and create from that raw material.

One of the most critical parts of a freelance writer's job is understanding context. What is the context of this company so that their copy can speak to their audience with a high level of nuance and thoughtfulness? How can we creatively position their brand voice? Or, what is the context of this person's entire life so we can write a memoir that moves people?

AI will never (fully) understand context on a human level. If you're an Artisan Freelancer worth your salt, you have nothing to worry about, just the same way that the best illustrators weren't decimated by the invention of the photograph and theoretical mathematicians weren't replaced by calculators. You may even use some AI tools in your process, whether that's for research or outline creation, but they will never replace the need for highly-skilled writers and storytellers.[17]

---

17   For more on the state of artificial intelligence as it applies to freelancers, visit: <u>amysuto.com/six-figure-freelancer</u>

Until robots can feel as we do, AI-generated writing will land in an uncanny valley of "yeah, that looks like writing" but will ultimately feel empty. And if we do get to the point where robots can feel emotions—well, that's a whole other problem.

Automate Your Way to Freedom

Remember that list of my ten tasks from earlier in the chapter? I was able to automate and/or outsource all ten of those, which meant I got back **twenty-five hours per workweek**. That's **1,050 hours per year** in a forty-two-workweek year! (And yes, I think all freelancers should try and optimize their time to take ten weeks off per year—but that's for another chapter.)

Once you have robots do the heavy, monotonous lifting for you, what are you going to do with all that time? Are you going to spend more time with loved ones? Are you going to make pottery or build your eleven-thousand-piece Lego set of the world map that you'll throw darts at to determine your next adventure? Go see your favorite band in concert?

Personally, I love to travel and spend time off wandering about the world with friends and seeing family. In 2021, I spent three months in Europe working remotely and took plenty of time off to take pasta making lessons in Milan, and enjoy an eight-course tasting menu in Budapest.

But what about those tasks that robots can't do? In the next chapter, I'll show you how to hire and work effectively with a virtual assistant.

Amy's Field Notes: Robots are Doing My Job Right Now

As I write this, robots are working for me. Ones and zeros are customizing and sending my cold emails, sending invoice reminders to my clients, and creating and rescheduling meetings on my calendar. I wouldn't be able to write this book without these automation tools doing parts of my freelancing job for me.

I have people helping me, too: my bookkeeper is doing my books, my lawyer is helping me with some paperwork, and my proofreader is editing one of my blogs. My graphic designer is working on a new landing page, and I'm about to meet with a web developer who is going to help me with some of my website elements.

When people ask how I "do it all," the answer is that I don't do it by myself. Right now, I have a small team of people and automation tools keeping everything moving along.

I go a step further and automate other parts of my life, too: my groceries are delivered to my doorstep, I order what I need online rather than go to a store, and my personal trainer updates my fitness app with workouts I have to do that week and holds me accountable.

Automations and outsourcing are the only way you'll be able to scale your freelancing business. Your systems need to work for you: not the other way around.

Once you're making more money, it's up to you to buy back your time while you still have it.

PART 3: HOW TO LAND BETTER, HIGHER-PAYING CLIENTS

CHAPTER 22:
HIRE AND WORK EFFECTIVELY WITH A VIRTUAL ASSISTANT

I used to be an assistant in Hollywood as my full-time job. While I found Hollywood to (generally) be a not-so-great work environment, I did work for a few great people who taught me a lot about what it means to work smarter, not harder.

When it came time for me to hire a full-time virtual assistant to help with what I needed done, I was able to pull from a lot of my experience doing the role to create frameworks to work effectively with my virtual assistant.

Full disclosure: I no longer work with a virtual assistant, but that's simply because I instead hire researchers, proofreaders, editors, book-keepers, and other specialists on a freelance basis to do what I used to have a virtual assistant do. Depending on what your freelance workload looks like and if/how you want to scale your freelancing, you may want to hire both a virtual assistant and specialists, or just one or the other. We'll cover outsourcing to specialists more in the next chapter, but for now, let's talk about virtual assistants specifically.

When to Hire a Virtual Assistant

It's 10am on a Tuesday. You're about to dive into a day of back-to-back meetings, and you've got three startups breathing down your back: each one wants quick turnarounds (by end of day!) with new copy to be written, and they're all willing to pay rush fees to get their deliverables done fast. You've also just finished writing an eBook for a client, but you don't have the time to proofread. Oh, and what about that payment that's supposed to come in from a client who had you invoice their billing department? Did they get your bank details? How can you handle all of this when you're going to be on eight video calls today?

Answer: you can't. You're at a fork in the road: you can either raise your rates to decrease the number of clients you have, which will increase your earnings and reduce your frantic state, or you can hire a virtual assistant.

In fact, you might even want to do both. That way, you can get more time and space with higher rates, and that additional revenue can go to hiring a virtual assistant to take over the busy work you don't want to do.

If you've finally gotten over-booked and busy, it's time to create a path to scaling. Scaling your freelance business looks different depending on what your goals are, and if your goal is to build out a full-service marketing agency or even simply decrease the amount of busywork you have to do each week, hiring a virtual assistant can help with that.

How to Hire a Virtual Assistant

There are a few different ways to go about the hiring process when you're looking for your new partner-in-crime.

I've always found it easier to do the hiring myself: I started by hiring friends who needed work, and then began posting formal job postings on job platforms.

You have three options when it comes to hiring a virtual assistant:

- **Hire a 1099 freelancer.** You can keep things simple by hiring freelance talent from a freelance platform, and making sure your hired freelancer has good reviews and a track record. Remember, there are legal guidelines when it comes to hiring freelance talent: your virtual assistant can be assigned tasks by you, but you can't control a) how they work b) when they work. So, if you need a virtual assistant to log on at a certain time and be available when you need them to be, that's not a freelancer. That's an employee. You don't want to get in trouble with the law when it comes to freelancer misclassification, so be sure to consult with a lawyer when adding to your team.

PART 3: HOW TO LAND BETTER, HIGHER-PAYING CLIENTS

- **Hire a company.** There are companies that offer virtual assistant services, and you can hire them to handle the sourcing of a virtual assistant. If something goes wrong, they can also connect you with a new assistant. This can be helpful as most of these candidates (ideally!) are vetted and trained by the company itself, so there's a standard of quality that's being ensured compared to taking a risk on a random freelancer.

- **Hire an employee.** When I hired a virtual assistant, I hired them as a full-time employee through my company with the help of a lawyer and accountant. We got them set up on payroll and all that jazz. Workers' comp and general liability policies are also usually required, depending on the laws in your state. Getting your employee set up properly does require professional help in order to make sure you're staying compliant with everything, so don't skimp on this.

No matter how you hire a virtual assistant, you've still got to pick someone who gels with you and the way you work!

When it's time to interview candidates, make sure you're clear on their job description. What are your expectations for them? Are they working for you on a freelance basis, or part-time or full-time? When do they need to be available for tasks? Are they pleasant and do they seem trustworthy?

I recommend asking some (if not all!) of the below questions in an interview:

- What do you like about being a virtual assistant?
- Tell me about your resume. What was your favorite past employer/client to work for?
- What do you not enjoy about your work?
- Can you share with me a time where something went wrong, and how did you handle it?
- If I asked for your help on [a typical task you would need help with], how would you go about completing it?
- Is being a virtual assistant a stepping stone to another path? If so, where do you want to go?
- What is one thing you're looking to improve about the way you work?

These questions can help you get a sense of if someone has a good attitude, or is just doing this job for a quick buck, or if they're detail-oriented and motivated by helping others.

Remember, this virtual assistant will probably be handling some sensitive documents such as credit card information or other details you'll need to loop them into so they can help you. It's important to get a sense of what motivates them and if they're going to be a good team member.

When You Make Hiring Mistakes

As my freelance career was starting to take off, I had hired a virtual assistant who had met with me right after she graduated, and she seemed to care about the things I did, and she was hungry for work. She was in-between assistant jobs, and I was in need of a new virtual assistant. So, I called her up, and offered her an hourly wage that was above what most post-graduate assistants were making with no experience, and she accepted.

However, when she saw how much I was making, she started to turn sour. Why wasn't she getting paid more?

What she didn't see, of course, was that by the time I hired her I was four years into my freelancing career. I had worked crazy hours to get to a place where I could make quite a bit of money, and I had hired a full team of editors and proofreaders at that point to help with different freelance projects. I was also investing in art projects made by friends of mine, so the money I was making was not just paying for my expenses, it was being spent on storytelling I wanted to support and make real. I also gave out regular bonuses to team members who were going above and beyond (I still do!) and her compensation was fair and what she agreed to before starting with me.

That assistant just grew even more sour, and her work deteriorated even as I tried to loop her into creative projects to help her feel emboldened and part of more fun things instead of just admin work. I eventually had to fire her, but didn't do so quickly enough.

You're going to make hiring mistakes. The adage of "hire slow, fire fast" is something to take to heart. Business isn't personal (which can create a sticky situation if you hire friends or family) but we're humans, so even if you're letting someone go because they clearly don't want to do a role anymore, they're still going to feel the bitter sting of rejection.

Understand this and be the bigger person. Always stay polite, centered, and fire people quickly so they can find the environment that is a better fit for them. The biggest lesson I've learned with hard things is to handle them as they come: don't ignore them or hope they'll resolve themselves on their own. The monster and anxiety of the situation will just grow bigger and more complicated the more you turn away from it. The weed sucks the life out of the garden it is allowed to grow in.

When hiring an assistant, start with a test period (either a single assignment or a fixed period of time) and make sure your potential assistant knows this is a trial time designed for you both to see if it's a good fit.

After you hire someone, make sure you've created systems that reward them for great work, and keep them motivated even through the slog that is endless admin work. Bonuses and performance reviews can help, as admin work isn't the most exciting field. Bonuses can reinforce great work, and performance reviews can offer areas to improve.

If you decide to work with friends and family, understand that you're risking that relationship. Great friendships can lead to great working relationships, but if you and that person aren't aligned then things can get sticky. I love working with people I know who I respect, but I've also lost friendships because I realized that people don't prioritize work or creative collaborations in the way that I do. So, just be aware of the risks you're taking on when working with friends in any capacity.

I don't mean to scare you off of hiring virtual assistants! I've also worked with virtual assistants who made my life easier and were a joy to work with. Just take the hiring process seriously and make sure you have a good contract in place if things go wrong.

Ways Freelance Writers Can Work Effectively with Virtual Assistants

When I was working as an assistant in Hollywood, the biggest barrier to doing my job well was a boss who couldn't communicate or wasn't approachable when I had questions I needed answered.

The same goes for your virtual assistant. Realize that you'll probably need to be more hands-on in the beginning as your assistant gets to know what you need help with. Any learning period to be proficient and get a handle on a job is about three months. Don't ask me why, but it's almost a law of physics. If someone hasn't caught on by then and made things easier for you, they never will.

As a freelance writer, you're going to want to get clear on how your virtual assistant can help you. They could assist with research, proofreading, or even with invoicing and contract management (but make sure you have final approval of any contracts before they get sent out!)

When it comes to financial stuff, I generally recommend outsourcing that to a business manager instead, but some freelancers prefer to have their virtual assistant handle everything.

Another area your virtual assistant comes in handy is with client outreach. As I mentioned in the example in the last chapter, your virtual assistant can save you dozens of hours just by taking over all of your potential client outreach: they can submit proposals for you on freelance platforms, they can help you with sending cold reach-outs, and they can even research potential clients you might be able to work with.

You can also have your virtual assistant cultivate a daily digest of interesting news for you, or do a round-up of new podcasts worth listening to in your niche. Get creative and consider all of the things that are both "necessary" and "nice to have" and prioritize your virtual assistant's to-do list accordingly.

In terms of best practices, here are some of my top tips when it comes to working with virtual assistants:

- **Set weekly meetings with your virtual assistant.** If your assistant is a full-time employee, consider daily meetings in the beginning. If they're part-time, maybe meet 2-3 times per week. Or, if you're working with a freelancer, try meeting with them once per week. As you continue to work together, you'll be able to reduce the number of times you meet with them or the length of your meetings.

- **Create a collaborative to-do list with deadlines.** One of the key parts of working with a virtual assistant is making sure you're on the same page as them when it comes to deadlines and deliverables. You can create a collaborative to-do list or project center in a project management tool, or you can keep it simple with a shared to-do list app. No matter what platform you use, make sure your assistant gets reminders when deadlines are approaching, and that you can both add items to the to-do lists. After a call with your virtual assistant, make it a habit that they add any new to-do list items to their shared list within an hour after the call so you know they're on it. That way, you can prevent missed deadlines or unclear requirements. Deadlines are essential to getting things done: thinking someone is going to accomplish something as fast as they can almost never works because their motivation is not yours. They aren't driving the business: they are doing what they're being told to do.

- **Audit what you're outsourcing each week.** Do you still have too much on your plate? Are there other things your virtual assistant could do to help you? Outsource as much as you can: if you've taken the time to hire and train a virtual assistant, they should be helping you get to a place where you're not having to sweat the small stuff.

- **Two can be better than one.** Before deciding that a virtual assistant isn't working out for you, may want to consider if hiring someone else can help. One virtual assistant may only be able to do their tasks about 70% as well as you would do if you were handling the tasks on your own. (It's your business after all, you care more!) But if you hire two virtual assistants who both can do their jobs 70% as well as if you were doing the tasks yourself, then you've got 140% competency which is an improvement on you running yourself ragged and never outsourcing anything. However, don't just use hiring someone else as a band-aid solution if your first assistant isn't working well with you or handling their workload well.

- **Understand the difference between personal tasks and business tasks.** If you know from the jump you want your virtual assistant to handle personal tasks like booking concert tickets and dinner reservations for you, make sure they know in advance what they're signing up for. Some assistants prefer to only work on business tasks, and others are okay doing both. Personal assistants are generally paid at a lower rate than business-focused assistants (but not always!) and this stigma is especially true in cities like LA and NYC where high-income households often have a "first assistant" who handles their business admin work, and a "second assistant" who handles their personal errands and reservations. As a former first assistant, I dreaded handling personal tasks, as they felt like they were higher stakes and didn't really drive my boss' business forward. While this stigma doesn't ring true for most virtual assistants, just make sure you're transparent about the types of tasks you'll need help with in your job description.

- **Evaluate your virtual assistant's bandwidth.** As you work with a virtual assistant, you may see their job performance dip over time. It's natural for freelancers and employees to have periods of time where they struggle, just keep an eye out for the signs they're burned out or have too much on their plate—particularly if they are full-time employees. Most of us over-perform when we get started at a new job, and then settle into our normal work ethic. If your virtual assistant is getting sloppy, it might be because they are losing motivation, not able to handle the tasks you're giving them, or they have something going on in their personal life. It's up to you to check in and see what's going on. From there, you have a few choices: find a new virtual assistant with a higher bandwidth, give your virtual assistant some time off, or reduce their workload. If the value they're bringing is starting to slide, it might not make financial sense to keep them on. This happened with a virtual assistant I was working with, and after trying to accommodate her for a few months and get to the root of the problem, I eventually had to let her go and figure out how to automate every part of her job. This is part of the reason I don't work with virtual assistants as much anymore, but I'm also not looking to scale into an agency model.

Overall, virtual assistants can be awesome assets to you and your freelance writing work. They can help you get back more time, grow your freelancing, and transition into an agency model if that makes sense for you and your interests.

Amy's Field Notes: The One-Year Turnover Rule

I've hired dozens and dozens of people for a variety of different roles. I've hired web designers, graphic designers, editors, proofreaders, assistants—the list goes on. That's why when I find someone I love working with, I pay well and give them incentives to stick around.

Something happens when the year mark hits, though. Almost every freelancer I've worked with gets to the year mark of working with me and my team, and then the work starts to suffer in ways that can't be ignored.

I don't blame people: after doing anything for a year, it might be time for a change. The high-intensity need to impress a new boss is strong at the beginning. You burn bright. But then over time? It's easy to get comfortable. And the thing with things that burn twice as bright? They last half as long.

The humans you hire aren't robots, so understand their motivation will come and go in waves. Either ride out the dips, maybe hire someone else to help, or look elsewhere for new talent.

PART 3: HOW TO LAND BETTER, HIGHER-PAYING CLIENTS

CHAPTER 23:
BUILDING A FREELANCING AGENCY

If you can't tell, I'm not a fan of the agency model. As an introverted freelance writer, I'm not a fan of being in a role where my day-to-day is focused on managing other people. Instead, I much prefer to be an individual craftsman, emerging from the cabin in the woods I'm staying in with a beautiful piece of copy in hand for my client to do with it what they will.

I prefer solo freelancing with occasional team support on researching and editing needs because it works best for what I want my ideal day-to-day to look like. My approach of writing in solitude with some support on more complex projects works best for me. I have more time to devote to things like writing this book, maintaining my blog, and writing my novel (coming out sometime in the next decade!)

However, if you love the opportunity to hang out on video calls and solve problems with other people *even more* than you love writing, the agency model can be a great model for you!

This book isn't going to teach you how to do that because it's not something I'm a fan of, but I'm sure you can find some awesome resources through the Internet search machine. But, I will share some basics as a retired veteran of the agency trenches.

What is an Agency?

An agency is a company that hires freelancers or employees to help accomplish client projects. An easy example of this would be an ad agency like the one featured in *Mad Men*, but you don't need to be a whisky-drinking Don Draper to head up a creative team and make things happen. Agencies can be copywriting focused, or they can be content focused. They can own the whole process from idea to execution of a deliverable like a video, or they can just deliver things like written branding materials.

The whole point of an agency is to be a collection of talent that can solve a client's problem faster and more efficiently than if that client had to hire out every role individually. Every agency will have its own list of services and be focused on a different niche. Some agencies will be more creative, others will be more tactical.

There are pros and cons of the agency model.

Pros of the agency model:

- You can scale your business quickly and provide a ton of value to clients.
- You can work on interesting, fast-paced projects and own the whole thing.
- You can put your creative direction to work, and help the client from start to finish.
- Your income becomes more passive as you're monetizing other people's time, not just your own.
- You have the potential (but aren't guaranteed!) to make a lot more money than as a solo freelancer.

Cons of the agency model:

- Great talent at an affordable rate is hard to find.
- People are inconsistent, and if you're hiring freelancers, they might not be available when you need them.
- Full-time employees can get expensive and eat into profits if you have a slowdown in clients.
- If someone in your agency turns in bad work, it's up to you to problem-solve and hire a replacement and pay a rush fee to meet a deadline.
- Your work is directly tied to the project's results, not just your individual performance.
- You'll spend less time as a writer, and more time as a people manager.

A word of warning on agencies: you may find a slew of influencers on social media who are trying to convince you that running an agency is the easiest job in the world. You hire people, they do all the work, you keep all the profit! You just need a team of virtual assistants and the cash machine keeps printing.

If someone's telling you that you can make easy money, they're probably making easy money off of you. They're probably selling you an expensive course or coaching program, not a feasible business model. You can't pop bottles in the club if your virtual assistants keep turning over or if your company missed a deadline for a client. Recruiting great, reliable talent is harder than you think. (When I failed at starting my own agency, my partner and I had reviewed over 100,000 applications for writers… and interviewed less than 1% of those applications.)

Walk into every new business venture with your eyes wide open so you know what it takes to succeed—and whether or not the sacrifices are worth what's waiting on the other side.

Tips for Running an Agency

I'll share my story at the end of this chapter about how I (failed!) to build a successful copywriting agency so you can learn from my mistakes. In the meantime, here are some tips I learned in the process of researching how agencies work, how to build them, and what to do (and not to do!)

- **Be clear with your clients on what you offer.** Your agency should have a clear niche. My recommendation is to keep your agency laser-focused. If you try to do everything at first, you'll probably fail. However, if you niche down to a particular set of services like owning the self-publishing process from idea to book marketing, you're in a much better position to deliver great results and become an expert in your field.

- **Pay your freelancers fairly.** You can pay freelancers on a per project or per hour basis. I know agency owners can have different approaches, such as sharing a set percentage of the project budget with their freelancers. Pick the model that is fair and ethical based on what your workflow is.

- **Pay your agency freelancers even when you get stiffed.** An hour worked should always be an hour paid. You as the agency manager take on the risk of the project: that's not the case with those working for you. Always uphold your contracts and pay people what you promise.

- **Have your agency freelancers sign NDAs.** Make sure all of the freelancers or employees you have doing work on a project have signed NDAs with your freelancing company. That way, they can be held liable in case they leak confidential client information. It's also important your freelancers have professional liability insurance if something like this happens. (It's important that everyone has professional/general liability, but you should make it mandatory with any freelancers you hire.)

✷ Quick Tip: Solve More Problems for Your Agency Clients

Not sure what services to add to your agency offerings? Go back through your messages with clients and see what services they were asking for. Or, conduct a survey of your current clients and see what other services they need help with.

At the end of the day, even if you don't scale into a full-on agency, freelancing doesn't have to be a completely solo profession. My business partner Kyle plays an integral role in my work, and he has helped me ideate on how to grow my freelance business. I owe him so much for his wisdom and support.

I'm also so grateful for the freelancers who help me with things like proofreading this book, designing this book's cover and interior, and all of the other amazing folks who help me with projects when I need their different skillsets and perspectives.

In essence? Find what works for you and go from there.

Amy's Field Notes: My Failure to Build a Copywriting Agency

I love talking about failure, because it's a treasure trove of lessons. So, here's a recent failure: my failure to build out a copywriting agency.

I created this company called Kingdom of Ink with my partner Kyle. Together, we vetted and brought on a team of writers who we proudly put on our website. We created a "mutual aid" mechanism: meaning, a percentage of each successful project would be shared amongst the entire group of writers. That meant one person's win would be everyone's win, and we hoped that would create an atmosphere of shared learning, support, and community. We would operate as the platform, helping to gather leads, foster community, and empower our freelancers to take charge of their careers with our support behind them.

Boy, we were so wrong.

When the clients started coming in, we started assigning projects to people. However, our writers had some trouble maintaining deadlines, and weren't acing the meetings like we'd hoped. So, my partner Kyle took a more active role in meeting with clients, but they didn't want to meet with the writers directly. They wanted us to be the middleman, which didn't fit with our model. That would be too much of a game of telephone.

Then came the issue of what happened when a project went wrong, and this killed our company.

One of our writers dropped the ball with a prickly client, and basically ghosted them. Suddenly, that client was blowing up my phone in the middle of the night, despite the fact that it was our writer's client, not mine. This wasn't the deal we made: our writers were supposed to take ownership over their projects and clients, not shuffle off angry people to me and moonwalk out of their obligations.

After the project was handled and I mediated the situation, Kyle and I sat down and looked at the numbers. The agency wasn't making enough to justify the amount of time it was requiring from both of us, so we shut it down.

I'm much happier being a solo freelancer these days. All my projects are my own, and I'm not depending on other people to deliver or make clients happy. My years of experience with clients has given me superpowers in conflict resolution, and I know how to deliver on my own promises.

If you decide to start an agency, know that you're also handing over your trust in other people. Your trust will be broken, and you'll have to learn the ins and outs of what it means to manage other people to get the best work out from them—all while keeping the project under budget.

This isn't to say an agency model done right can't be successful. I've seen others build it, and I saw the changes I would have had to make in order to make my agency succeed. But the difference was that I wasn't willing to become a full-time people manager. I much prefer my cozy days spent writing with minimal management.

Failure has taught me more than success ever has, so lean into your mistakes and let them light the way to a better tomorrow.

PART 3: HOW TO LAND BETTER, HIGHER-PAYING CLIENTS

CHAPTER 24:
HOW TO LEVEL UP YOUR WRITING SKILL

I've spent most of this book talking about what most freelancers are weak on: the business side of freelancing.

But what about the work itself? The magic of the written word?

When it comes to honing your writing skill, it's all about combining theory with 10,000 hours of practice. You become a better writer by reading more, writing more, and analyzing how to hit the moving target of what clients want. Even the way you present your finished documents can affect how a client views your writing—but like I said, this chapter is just about the words.

Books to Improve Your Writing

All types of reading improve your writing. Reading the news, personal essays, even social media posts (to a degree!) can improve your vocabulary and word choice. It can also help you learn more about what writing lights that fire within you—and what puts you to sleep.

But when it comes to good ol' fashioned craft, here are the books I recommend[18] you read (and re-read!) to hone your craft:

---

18   To get my full list of book recommendations, visit: amysuto.com/six-figure-freelancer

- **The Artist's Way by Julia Cameron.** Even if you're a technical copywriter, there's still artistry to be found in your work. I love *The Artist's Way* because I believe, without exception, we are all artists at heart.

- **The Adweek Copywriting Handbook by Joseph Sugarcane.** This is a great resource for copywriters looking to sharpen their copywriting craft.

- **Building a Story Brand by Donald Miller.** One of my favorite books to recommend to new freelance writers. If you work anywhere adjacent to marketing, this book is a must-read. There's a lot of great ways you can weave storytelling into your work, even for your own marketing materials as a freelancer.

- **The Elements of Style by Strunk & White.** This is such a critical read for writers of any kind. Grammar is such an undervalued skill in the world of spell-checking tools, but let me tell you it's ~critical~ for you to master if you expect people to pay you for your words.

- **Elements of Eloquence by Mark Forsyth.** This book changed the way I write. It was given to me as a gift and I can credit so many breakthroughs in my craft to this handbook on eloquence.

It's critical that you read related (and unrelated!) books to your niche. A poetry book might contain something that inspires you to write a tagline differently. A business book might help you structure your own freelancing business better. A New York Times profile piece might inspire you to write a client's bio in a way that's more engaging.

As a memoir ghostwriter, I try to consume memoirs so that I can leverage my knowledge when I write memoirs for people so they get a book that feels modern and utilizes all the tricks modern memoirists use to abridge memories and generate a compelling book.

The experience of reading is undervalued in today's video- and photo-forward world. That's why making reading a daily habit will help you stand out in a crowded marketplace.

Learning How to Write for Clients

Another key aspect of honing your craft as a freelance writer is understanding what your client actually wants in the first place. Take the time to ask questions so you can understand their taste. "Good writing" is subjective, and dependent on your client's *why*. Why are they building their business? What's their mission and their goal that drives them? If a client comes to me to rewrite their biotech company's homepage, their website is going to probably be a lot less voice-y compared to someone coming to me to rewrite their party planning startup.

Here's the information you want to get before starting a project:

- What is the purpose of this piece of copy/this memoir/this blog post? What desired emotions/actions do you want your ideal customers/readers to have?

- What are some of your favorite pieces of writing that are similar to what you're trying to accomplish? What are some examples of writing you want to avoid?

- How fun/witty can this copy be? What are some examples of tone/voice that you love, or want to avoid?

- Do you want this copy to be concise and punchy, or long and thoughtful? What is your ideal length?

These questions will help you hone in on what your client wants more quickly. When they send over comps for their project, take the time to read through them and analyze what the client likes about other websites/books/projects and their copy. Remember that you're the expert, not the client, so even if they send you some ideal copy examples, what they *actually want* might be buried underneath the surface.

If they send you a polished, millennial-facing startup's website but want their copy to be chaotically funny and re-focused to Gen Z's "unique" sense of humor, the example they sent you will probably only inform you of the type of approach and feeling they're going for, not the actual execution.

Your job as a writer is to look beyond what they *think* they want, and to give them what they *really* want. This isn't the case for every client, as some founders with marketing backgrounds will have a stronger sense for what they want. But as you become an expert freelance writer in any niche, you'll be able to read the tea leaves your client wasn't even thinking of so it feels like it checks all their boxes.

This goes a bit beyond craft and into customer service, but it still stems from a place of knowing your niche and what makes a written deliverable successful.

Same thing goes with memoir/nonfiction freelance ghostwriters: we've got to understand the books that our clients love and why they love them (everyone and their mother will always point to *Eat Pray Love* in the memoir space since it's so widely known) but it's up to us to have read more niche books that employ structures that we can borrow from and that better fit our clients' stories.

This comes back to reading widely. If you read widely, you'll have more tools at your disposal to write better copy and to also send references to your clients to get to their desired end result with higher accuracy.

Example Landing Page: Meet Traitor Jen

If I had more free time and a few billions of dollars to spare (hello, investors!) then I'd start an ethical grocery delivery company that runs on crypto and cuts small businesses in on the profits. Sound epic? I know, it is.

Now, I'm going to use this fake company I've mentioned a few times in this book to show you two different versions of a landing page. The first will be a bad example, and the second will be the homepage for my imaginary startup that is sure to net gazillions and help customers all over the globe.

After you read both, I'll break down the difference between the two.

Example: Bad Version of a Landing Page (Typos Incoming!)

TRATOR JEN

Traitor Jen
Better grocery delivery.

PART 3: HOW TO LAND BETTER, HIGHER-PAYING CLIENTS

[ABOUT]
Hi there, we are traitor jen, we help people get their groceries faster than ever before. We offer our customers flexible pricing, lots of different options, and we also provide great connections with local businesses so you can get what you want when you want it. We have our own couriers because we are a co-op and they get part of the profits. Just download the app, order some stuff, and we'll get it to your door. We're run by a founder who came from the startup world and for some reason a bucket of money showed up on her door and now she started traitor jens. welcome.

[CTA]
Download our app.

Shop With Us

There's a lot of apps out there, so honestly, thank you for picking ours. We offer free delivery on your first orders, we deliver nationwide, and we take requests if a store is out of something. We also accept BTC and ETH. If you have referred friends, you are eligible for referral bonuses.

[CTA]
Download our app.

Example: The Better Version of the Landing Page

Web Copy Prepared for Traitor Jen
version one, [date]

Traitor Jen
Delivery that does good.

[ABOUT]
Groceries and other goods delivered from your favorite local shops.
We sell the good stuff, without selling out.

Sure, the idea of "selling out" is very Gen. X of us. Quaint, even. But take a look around: the whole world's covered in, like, the same six brands. Which: good on you — you conquered commerce! Still, some of us enjoy a little more personality with our purchases.

That's what Traitor Jen is for: defying the big-box despots by making it easier to shop with your favorite local, independently-owned stores.

Need to snag a zucchini from the little produce market down the way? New board game just came into your favorite hobby shop? Could really use some Ibuprofen for that wicked hangover? Order from up to 4 unique mom'n'pop spots within a 5-mile radius of your home for a single fee — and have it delivered in 2 hours or less.

You need it? We know some people who've got it:
- Grocery stores
- Farmers' markets
- Convenience stores
- Pharmacies
- Hobby and craft stores
- Bookstores, record stores, and comic book shops

[CTA]
Get the small business hookup.
Shop local, go bankless.

The Name's 'Traitor Jen' — But We'll Never Betray You

Unlike other national grocery delivery apps, we're all about empowering local business owners and drivers, not exploiting them. We pay our drivers a living wage through profit-sharing organized by smart contracts on the blockchain, and we give independent shops a humane way to compete with the ruthless delivery models of the major players.

PART 3: HOW TO LAND BETTER, HIGHER-PAYING CLIENTS

Don't get it twisted: The only people who can't trust us are the chain stores steamrolling every strip mall in sight.

What's in it for You?
Traitor Jen is available in major metropolitan areas across all 50 states. If the prospect of easy delivery from the best small businesses in town isn't enough to get you on our side, allow us to spice up the offer:

- **Free delivery on your first 5 orders**, plus 2 free insulated tote bags made from recycled plastic sourced by The Ocean Cleanup.
- **Free delivery on ANY order over $80**, period. Forever.
- **We take requests.** Tack on a custom pit stop and our drivers will make it happen, even if it's not in the app yet.
- **Go bankless.** Yeah, we're taking on the banks, too. We accept crypto payments in BTC and ETH.
- **We have a heart, too.** Ten percent of our gross profits go to charities like Feeding America, FINCA International, and Habitat for Humanity.
- **Hook up your friends** and get $100 in delivery credit for every new account referral.

[CTA]
What you want, from the businesses you want to support.
Get it delivered.

Download the Traitor Jen app on Google Play or the Apple App Store today.

The Difference Between Bad and Great Landing Pages

The differences between the two landing pages are, of course, stark:

- **The bad version is vague in its language:** its tagline "better grocery delivery" could apply to any app out there. Better compared to *what*? Overall, the first landing page example lacks specificity, is boring to read, and doesn't deliver (haha) the information to our doorstep in a very efficient way.

- **The bad version speaks in passive language** like "if you have referred friends, you are eligible for referral bonuses" rather than active language such as "refer friends for a bonus."

- **The good version is well structured.** Even without a design, you can imagine how the flow of this landing page will look, and it's incredibly readable.

- **The Call-to-Actions (CTA's) are varied yet concise in the good version.** Keeping buttons and call-to-action copy simple yet still in the voice of your brand is tricky. This second version does a great job of that.

- **The good landing page is value-driven: the bad version is just listing stuff.** A good landing page understands that the customer wants to know, "what's in it for me?" as soon as possible.

- **This is a damn good startup idea.** If any founders want to run with this business idea, hit me up. I'd be happy to sell this and the marketing materials to you for a few bucks in exchange for you changing the world. Cool?

Grow From Client Feedback

The clearest form of client feedback will come from whether or not they re-hire you to do a job. If they part ways after the first project, it could mean they don't have the budget to hire you, or they didn't think you were a good fit. (Or, they just don't have any more writing needs!)

On occasion, you'll have clients that outright do not like your work. Some of this feedback is valuable if it's constructive, while some of it is not if they're just trying to get free work from you or are trying to complain to get out of paying you.

Or maybe you didn't match the right style for the type of copy the client was looking for. Maybe you let your Faulkner flag fly a little too high for this landscaping website, when they really needed your best Don Draper. It happens: that's why freelance writing pays so well when you're an expert writer. Understanding and implementing client needs is a skill in itself!

If you do get constructive feedback (especially if it's in-between drafts as you're doing revisions!) take note of what feedback you get repeatedly. See if there are areas to grow or improve on, and try to set aside your ego and see if a note is coming from a place of taste (a client's preferences) or craft (a sentence landing weird or sounding funny, or a piece of copy that is too verbose when they asked for something concise.)

If you find yourself consistently landing longer-term clients, or clients who hired you in the past come back to hire you for short-term projects, this is a very good sign. Take this as feedback that you're growing and succeeding in hitting the mark.

If you find yourself struggling to land work, don't panic. It just might mean you need to spend some more time learning, reading, and honing your craft, and adding more samples to your portfolio.

Never Stop Learning

As a freelance writer, it's key to keep learning—even as the jobs are rolling in. Create daily habits that keep you reading, learning, and practicing. Write on your blog, post on social media, and read books and articles that inspire you.

In the next part of this book, I'm going to dive into how to make your life as a freelancer sustainable to the point where you can create the lifestyle of your dreams. You'll learn what to do if work slows down or if you get burnout, how to think about passive income and other sources of active income, and how to create routines that support you when clients keep calling so you can work less and live more.

Amy's Field Notes: You Are What You Read

Words are like tchotchkes. They cling to your vocabulary like clutter on your desk. Even though I'm a digital nomad, I still have a tiny stone head the size of an eraser my brother gave me from his trip to Italy (it's good luck or something) and a fancy hand sanitizer dispenser that's cube shaped (I love cube-shaped things, and miss the days where cell phones used to be square, too.)

Your vocabulary and the way you write isn't yours: it's inherited. You learn how to do stuff, of course (like vary sentence length) but it's the delight of reading something great that contributes the most.

I took this great class at USC called *Writing to Be Read*. Does that sound like an obvious class title? Don't all writers write to be read? Well, the great writers do. That's why they're the top of their field: they take care in crafting the reader's experience. The average writer writes for themselves—and they overlook the reader's experience entirely.

If you want to write for yourself, start a diary. If you want to be paid for your words by other people, you have to put the time in to hone your craft.

There are no shortcuts to becoming a great writer. You can't "hack" it. Just like learning an instrument or training for a marathon, the key to success is in repetition... and reading works from those you admire.

If you want to be great at writing threads on social media, follow the top writers on that platform. If you want to be an expert at memoirs, pick up some best-selling autobiographies.

You are what you read, so pick wisely.

CHAPTER 25:
VALUE-BASED PRICING AND PACKAGES

There are so many freelance gurus out there who say things like "this is the one thing that 10x'd my income!!" or "do this to land dream clients!!" and most of their tips I found pretty useless. (And usually gatekeep-y as they then want you to watch their live seminar or book a call with them to actually hear what their tips are.)

However, there was one structural change to my pricing as a freelance writer that actually did triple my annual income and give clients more value, so please excuse me if I sound like I'm about to knock on your door wearing a pinstripe suit and a briefcase full of watches.

In 2021, I worked pretty much only on an hourly basis. This worked for me at the time because I was able to jump into creative projects for as long as they needed me, and peace out when the project was either completed or abandoned (which happens quite a bit in some of the niches I was working in.) I was also able to be generous with my copywriting clients—they were paying for my time, after all, so I was happy to do any number of revisions or extra research they needed. In this pricing model, I was optimizing for simplicity, and also preventing anyone from taking advantage of my time.

However, most clients want to be clear on the budget for a project before starting. This is totally understandable, but until 2022, I didn't quite know how to service these clients without getting locked into a project that would go on forever. I needed a fixed-rate pricing structure that could work both for myself and my clients.

Enter: package pricing. Basically, if you're a freelance writer in any niche, you can create a package of services or deliverables so that you can more easily budget your time and energy, and provide value to clients.

By listening to what my clients wanted and also finding a structure and price point that allowed me to be generous with my time and revisions, I hit the highest-earning months of my freelance career.

Here's how:

What is Package Pricing?

Simply put, a "package" is a bundle of services. The goal with packaging all of these services together is to create value with a related set of services. An example of this could be a social media content package, where you write copy for multiple social media channels for your client each month. You would then specify the word count for each channel, the number of revisions your client would have access to, and any other services you might include (such as scheduling the social media posts, responding to comments, or full account management.)

You can keep packages just focused on your writing services, or you can bundle adjacent services (like social media account management) which you can do yourself or outsource to a virtual assistant.

To sell a compelling package, you should aim to create the most value for your clients, and maybe even introduce them to services they wouldn't have thought of asking you for.

✶ Quick Tip: Pricing Your Packages

Confused on how to price your packages? Just break it down by the number of hours you anticipate each piece of the package will take, and then add 30% extra to the package. For example, if you're writing five social media posts per week for a client and you know it will take you ten hours per week at $100/hour, that's $1,000, and with the 30% extra, the final weekly total comes out to $1,300. If you want to provide discounts for larger packages, that could incentivize clients to spend a little more and take a risk on you.

How to 3x Your Income with Package Pricing

This pricing model is so great because it helps both freelancers and clients get what they want out of the working relationship.

Package pricing helps clients know exactly what they're getting for what cost, compared to hiring me on an hourly basis. I'm able to really dig into my freelance projects and make sure my clients are thrilled with the end result.

Package pricing helps freelancers because you're able to more clearly understand what your goals are for the year. Planning is easier when you know how to allocate the right amount of time to each client, rather than just maxing out your client roster when you're unsure how many hours you're going to bill for each project.

A great package can change your life when done right, so let's dive in!

3 Tips for Building Your Freelance Writing Packages

Tip #1: Get Specific on Your Deliverables

If your deliverables are vague, you and your clients might not be on the same page, which will lead to problems down the road.

So, get super specific on your deliverables, what they look like, and—when relevant!—provide examples before the project begins. Your deliverables could be a set of copywriting documents, a memoir manuscript, or whatever your freelance writing niche is.

Freelancers should set the terms for the deliverables: you should explain what you're offering and how the deliverables will look, rather than the client providing you the deliverable info. Any time the client is looking for something specific that's beyond a typical deliverable I've done in the past, I often opt to provide an hourly rate quote instead. This is especially true for creative projects that are a bit fuzzy when it comes to the scope of work. You can't create packages if you're not crystal-clear on the deliverables you're putting together.

Think of packages as pre-set terms. Kind of like when you walk into a sandwich shop and you can either make your own sandwich or buy from their pre-set special sandwich list. Your Veggie Surprise can have alterations, but generally, you're ordering it because the shop has dubbed it a high-quality combination of ingredients and secret sauces that you're going to love having for lunch.

Tip #2: Cap Word Count and Revisions

Always always *always* have an upper limit for your word count and a set number of revisions. This helps your client know how many revisions they have available, and encourages them to collate their notes (and their team's notes!) into one set of notes rather than doing endless revisions. This makes the process smoother on both sides, and keeps things moving at a good pace.

The last thing you want to do is get yourself into a bad situation of doing an infinite amount of work on a project. Instead, you can politely point to your contract with your client if they ask for more revisions, and recommend they switch to hourly with you beyond the agreed-upon limit.

If disagreements come up, it's important that these things are spelled out in writing in your contract. If you're on a freelance platform, be sure to write out your deliverable details in the messages so you have a record if something goes wrong.

Tip #3: Get Competitive with Your Rates So You Can Get Generous with Your Time

I always want to make sure I have the time, energy, and brain space to go above and beyond for my clients, and that's because I have competitive rates. If you're hiring the best, they should be highly skilled, well-rested, happy, and excited to give you some of their best thinking hours of their week—and those hours aren't cheap.

It's much harder to be generous when you're not taking care of yourself and consistently learning, resting, and making space for what you care about. Showing up inspired, excited, and ready to do great work requires a generous mindset.

That's why you need to charge more than what your first instinct is. When you're conceptualizing the scope of a project, it's important to over budget for time and energy so you can deliver great work, every time, but also don't get too crazy. You still need to back up the value behind what you're charging.

The Authentic Approach to Selling Freelance Packages

I don't believe in selling, at least not in the way you might think of it. I believe in creating compelling offerings, and finding and attracting the people who can benefit the most from them. Have confidence in your services, make sure they're discoverable, and the right people will find you.

Example: the tech community at large is great at moving fast, iterating, and building compelling products. I would also say a majority of the tech community is overdeveloped in building and undeveloped in communicating *why* what they are building is so great.

So, I jumped into the tech space to offer my creative and technical copywriting skills. I saw a need for my skills, and began to offer ways in which I could help.

The best packages solve a problem. And once you've found a problem to solve, you've got to spread the word to the people who need it the most.

Amy's Field Notes: Helping Small Business Owners

I love writing for entrepreneurs, and one of my packages helped a small business owner go from $0 to a bestselling product on Amazon. When I initially met her, she shared her vision with me for a consumer product that would help women. I realized her product should be demonstrated on social media, so I offered to not only write all of her copy but also to research and put together a strategy for her social media presence. I created a package for her that was my standard copy package with a slight twist to it to provide her the value I thought would help her the most. Months later, she had a successful launch and now has a bestselling product on Amazon!

Some of the best freelancers think outside the box to help their clients in different ways. In what ways can you create more value for your clients?

PART 4

BUILDING YOUR IDEAL LIFE AS A FREELANCE WRITER

PART 4: BUILDING YOUR IDEAL LIFE AS A FREELANCE WRITER

STORY #4:
PORTUGAL DAYDREAMS AS A DIGITAL NOMAD

Dispatches from a Freelance Writer's Life

I spent two months working remotely in Portugal, and to say it was an absolute dream is an understatement. From riding tuk-tuks up a mountain to visit Sintra's castles shrouded in mist, to traversing cobblestone streets to get delectable meals under $10 USD per person, I melt whenever I reminisce about our time in Lisbon and Porto.

Most people think my lifestyle is out of their reach, but that couldn't be further from the truth. It was ten times cheaper to spend two months in Portugal compared to any American city due to the currency exchange rate. Digital nomads can also travel even more on a budget, especially if you opt into hostels or co-living spaces that cater to traveling professionals. Being location-independent means you can live in cities when they're at their best, and skip town when you don't want to deal with a New York winter or an Arizona summer. You can mix and match cities that are expensive with places that are affordable to get the most out of your travel budget. You can orient your trip around conferences, seeing old friends, or concerts. In short? Total freedom and flexibility of lifestyle and budget.

That's not to say the digital nomad life is all sunshine and roses: the inconvenience of travel can take its toll, and you have to be thoughtful when designing your travel schedule.

As I write this, I'm on a flight back from London. I spent two weeks in England where I spoke at a conference, had a ton of great client meetings, caught up with old friends, and tried all the great vegan food with my partner Kyle.

While the two weeks were fun and productive (conferences are a great way to make new friends and meet potential clients!), I feel a bit rundown. Travel can do that to you, which is why you must balance the high-energy, go-go-go trips with the slower, let's-spend-a-month-somewhere-and-just-vibe trips.

If you choose the freelance life, you have the ability to design your life to suit your needs. You can travel as much or as little as you'd like. You have full control over your schedule: when you take meetings, when you're resting, and when you're in deep work times.

However, sometimes, staring at a blank slate with *so* much flexibility can be daunting. You might find yourself grappling with bad habits, an undisciplined mind, or a lack of motivation. Or, you might find yourself enjoying the freedom so much that you don't balance your life with enough deep work required to keep the quality of your work high.

I've experienced all of the above, and part of the work of becoming a six-figure freelancer is looking inward.

In this last part of *The Six-Figure Freelance Writer*, I'm going to go over the lifestyle changes and perspective shifts that you might need to make in order to live (and sustain!) your dream life.

CHAPTER 26:
USING MINDSET SHIFTS TO MAKE YOUR IDEAL LIFE A REALITY

Our minds are a powerful tool: when our minds freak out, our bodies generate stress chemicals. Adrenaline spikes, and we're in fight-or-flight mode.

When I started as a freelance writer, fear and stress ruled my life. I had worked two years of minimum-wage jobs in an expensive city, and I had never made enough money up until that point. That scarcity mindset affected me, and I often took on clients that didn't treat me with respect, and I didn't charge what my time was really worth. This kept me from finding the full roster of amazing clients that I have now.

The only thing that stands between you and your best self is… probably you. So, let's talk about the mindset shifts and changes you'll need to make to show up as the best version of yourself and attract your dream clients!

Auditing Your Habits

"You are what you do every day."

This inspirational quote is by (or I heard it from) Jon Chu, a film director I met (briefly) on the set of a far-less-inspirational Justin Bieber music video. His words stick with me to this day because your habits lead you down a path of success or a path of ruin. Your habits can make you happy, or they can make you the director of a music video populated with a bunch of badly behaved pop stars. Everyone's got their own priorities, fam.

At the beginning of my freelancing career, I didn't take my habits seriously. I thought discipline was for nerds and my focus (and income!) fluctuated on a daily basis. I was distracted by partying, dating, and all of the trappings of my early-twenties. I don't condemn my younger self: she just had different priorities—priorities that she didn't realize were sabotaging her chance at financial freedom.

It took a pandemic and an autoimmune disease for me to clean up my act, hit the books, and take a good hard look at my habits. I look at the moment I started leaning into healthy habits as the moment my freelance career skyrocketed, and you'll see the same thing when you start investing in yourself.

For the next week, I challenge you to write down the habits that are already a part of your day. What do you do? What do you eat? For each habit, write if it creates a positive, negative, or neutral charge to your life. Do you make your bed and that makes your room tidier? Or do you leave your dishes out all day which attracts bugs? (Guilty!)

The same goes for your work habits: are you reading nutritious books and news articles that contribute to growing your vocabulary and writing style? Or are you just scrolling on social media, which reduces your attention span? Are you writing regularly on your blog and newsletter?

After a week of habit auditing, pick one negative habit to replace with a positive one. Use a habit tracker (either an app or a simple pen-and-paper system) to track your progress on integrating this new positive habit in place of your negative one. Once you hit a 90% rate of sticking with the new habit, pick another bad habit to replace.

Changing your habits has a positive domino effect on your life, no matter where you start. For example, I wanted to start a habit where I sat out in the sun and spent time journaling every morning. Getting some sunshine improves my mood, which also improves my quality of work.

If I feel like I'm stressed out or not as far along in my work as I want to be, I start by auditing my habits using these questions:

- Do I have a meaningful community I'm a part of? What hobbies, events, or groups can I add to my week?
- Am I feeding my body what it needs every day? Do I have the right balance of fruit, veggies, and other whole foods and protein sources?
- Am I going on daily walks and integrating strength training and cardio

workouts into my schedule every week?
- Am I taking time to stretch, meditate, and journal?
- Do I spend time connecting with friends and family?
- Am I drinking enough water?
- Am I getting enough sunlight?
- Am I getting enough sleep?
- Do I seek out good books and other nourishing art and reading material that help me hone my craft and exercise my mind?
- Am I keeping my home and belongings clean and tidy?

This list is a good start to help you get a sense of areas you might be neglecting. I think you'll find that if you generate more awareness and energy around these pieces of life, other blocks in your life will also fall away.

Auditing Your Environment

Your environment affects how you're able to function. There are plenty of studies that show how a messy home creates a messy mind. Additionally, noises like airplanes flying overhead or traffic nearby can also affect how well you're sleeping or finding peace in your day-to-day.

Same goes with the people in your environment: if your roommate is a ball of anxiety and dread, you will probably be, too. We are the approximation of the five people we spend the most time with, so make sure your close friends and roommates are people you respect and aspire to be like—you're going to take on their traits and neuroses just by spending enough time with them, whether you like it or not!

As a freelancer, you also need to be self-motivated and driven. You don't have a boss telling you to show up at work every day—that's you!

This is why your environment is especially important. You don't need a fancy home office, but you do need a space where you can focus and find calm. If you've got noisy upstairs neighbors, "finding calm" might mean investing in a good pair of noise-canceling headphones. If you've got a messy spouse or roommate, it might mean moving your desk into a quiet, clean nook so you can have control over where you sit down to do work for the day.

In an ideal world, you'd be able to have a home office or co-working space where you can enforce physical work/life boundaries. As freelancers, we don't often have that luxury, so do what you can with what you have.

If you aren't sticking to a habit like eating well because you're surrounded by junk food, it may be time to enlist your household members to get healthy with you—or find a new method of storing junk food so it's not always tempting you.

If you're struggling to stay focused on your daily deep work as a freelancer, it might be because you have a number of distractions in your space. Consider changing your workspace, working from a coffee shop, or trying out a co-working space. While none of these are magic bullets, they could help revitalize your focus and reveal what you need to get things done.

You are your own boss, so make sure you're giving yourself every advantage you need to succeed.

Breaking Your Addiction to Negative Thought Patterns

The thing that held me back from being a full-time freelancer was letting myself get discouraged by my inner (negative!) monologue.

I can't charge that much. My time isn't worth it. My work isn't good enough.

I would think these thoughts even when I intellectually knew I was one of the best, most reliable freelance writers in my niche. These thoughts would plague my self-confidence even as my clients left glowing reviews and hired me again and again.

I'm not telling you to become arrogant and charge crazy rates just because: instead, I want you to weed out negative thoughts that keep you trapped in a cycle where you take on clients that don't respect you and don't pay you what your time is worth.

As a freelancer, it's key to retain a level of humility. You must be able to back up your rates and explain why you're charging what you're charging. You have to be able to point to past client testimonials and samples that show why you're the best at what you do. And if you're not there yet? You can adjust your rates accordingly.

However, you need the confidence to turn down abusive clients and jobs that have exploitatively low pay. You need the intuition to sniff out a scam. You're a lone warrior, someone with skills you leverage to help others. But you also need to protect yourself and your time, because no one else is going to.

To help quell negative thoughts, start your day by writing down things you're proud of. What accomplishments and little victories have you gotten lately? These can be internal validators: you can be proud of an assignment you finished, tickled by a turn of phrase you put in a blog post, and happy with your productivity the week before.

Get excited about the little wins under your control (not your clients'!) and continue to learn and improve as a freelancer. This will help you cement your confidence and keep you in the game so you don't get swept away by negative thoughts trying to sabotage you or keep you working for pennies.

When I unlocked my confidence, everything changed. When I had collected enough experiences that I felt like I was ready to charge a higher hourly rate beyond the $35/hour I started out at, I was able to find clients who also were able to pay that rate. This happened every time I raised my rates: my confidence in myself led my clients to have confidence in their decision to hire me.

Be your first and biggest fan. Don't let your ego outshine your experience, but instead own the value you bring to the table.

Attracting Wealth and Abundance

There's something that happens when you turn the corner from feelings of scarcity to feelings of abundance.

People treat you differently. As you let stress slide away, you hold your shoulders higher. You sit up straighter: you smile with a warmth of comfort. You stop being frenetic and stressed, and instead breathe deeper. You're more optimistic and it comes off in the first few minutes of a call with clients. They start to realize you're booked and busy—even if they're your only call for the day.

Instead of you desperately chasing them, they start to chase you. They realize you're a rarity: a freelancer who isn't worried and begging for their next gig. Instead, you're grounded, grateful, and in-demand.

Believe it or not, this attitude starts with an emotional shift within—it's not created from external validation. Happiness is an inside job. Freelancing is a people business, so the moment you become calm and at-peace with yourself and your environment, others can sense it, and they react accordingly. No one wants to work with someone who is scared and desperate. Everyone wants to work with the person who is happy and at peace with themselves: they want what you've figured out.

So, one of the greatest gifts you can give yourself as a mindset shift is to remind yourself that everything is going to work out. I recommend creating a vision board filled with images and mantras that represent your ideal future. Look at this vision board each day and meditate and journal as if all of those things are already here: that will help them materialize more quickly.

Some call this practice "manifestation": I think it's simply a good way to keep moving towards the future you want and calling those feelings to the present moment.

You have to back up all of these mindset shifts with action: they can't just be empty affirmations on a page. These positive thoughts and visualizations are meant to be your roadmap and your meditation focus that bring clarity to what action you need to take.

So, take a moment today and think to yourself:

I have everything I need.
I don't chase, I attract.
All the good things that belong to me, simply find me.

And take the time to sit with yourself and with the understanding that those good things are headed your way, as you've created the frameworks for them to arrive.

Amy's Field Notes: Retire the Alarm Clock

When you were an employee, your alarm clock helped you get up in the morning and out the door. It was a blaring reminder to get in your

"5-to-9" before your "9-to-5."

It's my belief you should ditch the alarm clock—let me explain why!

Part of the abundance mindset is believing that you have an abundance of time. Letting your body wake up at an intuitive time that's perfect for you is superior to getting your REM cycle wrecked by some screaming alarm clock.

To cultivate a sense of ease, calm, and peace, you should go to bed at a time that feels natural, and wake up when you're ready to seize the day. Do your best to not schedule morning meetings: those will only mandate you to set an alarm clock and they'll cut into your precious morning time to wake up and prepare for the day.

And the freedom of never having to wake up at a certain time? It will change your brain, provide you with the sleep your body deserves, and get you out of the "grind" mentality and instead challenge you to find a better, fully rested version of yourself.

PART 4: BUILDING YOUR IDEAL LIFE AS A FREELANCE WRITER

CHAPTER 27:
PREVENTING BURNOUT AS A FREELANCE WRITER

It's 4pm on a Friday and you're sprinting through an assignment you've been procrastinating on all week. You've been late to calls, letters are starting to spin on the page in front of you, and all words seem to have lost their meaning. You're crumbling under stress, feel consistently behind schedule, and collapse onto your couch all weekend (until Sunday night rolls around and you need to try and catch up on the work you didn't get done the week before!) You hang out with your friends less since you're so tired, and you don't have time for your hobbies and the things you care about.

If this feels like a constant state of your life rather than a rare circumstance, you, my friend, are *burned out*.

If you're operating from a scarcity mindset, you don't take days off for yourself to rest. You are always on, taking meetings and doing assignments on weekends, and pushing yourself until the pages blur in front of you.

You're not doing yourself any favors (or your clients/projects) by not having boundaries and taking your self-care seriously. When I was a new freelancer, I did this to myself on a weekly basis and I paid dearly for it. I kept getting into never-ending cycles of burnout until one day, I woke up and my finger joints were so swollen I couldn't type.

Ironically, I now only work fifteen to twenty hours per week on average depending on my project workload, and I've automated my systems so that I make even more than I did when I was a new freelancer breaking my body for fifty- to sixty-hour workweeks with no time off.

The moral of the story? If you're working all the time and harming your health, you're doing it wrong and your strategy needs to change, ASAP!

Signs You're Burned Out

Let's take a quiz!

Multiple Choice: you may be burned out if... (check all that apply)

- [ ] A: You feel a lack of motivation to do freelance or creative work
- [ ] B: You feel deeply exhausted in a way that goes beyond needing more sleep
- [ ] C: You feel overwhelmed to the point of hopelessness
- [ ] D: Depression and anxiety are quicker to take root in your day-to-day
- [ ] E: All of the above

Burnout can show up differently in all of us, but if you feel like any of the above apply to you, it may be time to take a step back from work and reset and refresh. Let's dive into some strategies to help you recover!

Thinking About Time Differently as a Freelancer

When I talk about working *smarter* not harder, I'm referring to what we've covered in early chapters when it comes to automating and outsourcing. You're probably a bad proofreader of your own work anyways (who isn't?) so why not hire a proofreader to catch any typos? Or a researcher who can help you bolster your work?

"But outsourcing costs money!"

For sure. So, start by just automating as much as you can.

"But setting up automations takes time!"

Do you know how much time you'll *save* by spending the extra time now to automate? Go back and review the automation chapter as a primer: great systems support you in the long run so that you can earn more and do better work. Follow the 80/20 rule: do the things that will take up 20% of your time to make your life 80% better.

"My clients want me to be available on the weekends, though."

Do all of your clients require that? If not, why not let go of the clients that want that time from you, and set expectations moving forward that you don't work on weekends? Otherwise, if weekend work is necessary, pick two days during the workweek that you are unavailable and make all of your clients aware you don't answer emails or do work those days. But what I've found is it's difficult to make exceptions without sustaining breaches in your fortress of rest. It's easier to hold strong on boundaries than to bend around everyone else's. There's always another job: if you don't prioritize your own well-being, no one else will.

If you don't rest, you'll get burned out and the quality of your work will suffer. A great adage I heard from a friend was "if you don't pick what day of the week you rest, your body will pick for you." And trust me, your body will make sure you get the rest you need, even if it has to force you to find the time. Don't get to that point: take care of yourself right now.

This is the easiest way in the world to impress clients and to prevent yourself from constantly being in a state of chaos.

Tools for Preventing Burnout

A book that changed my view on my work/life balance is *Burnout: The Secret to Unlocking the Stress Cycle* by Amelia and Emily Nagoski[19]. It helped me realize my workaholism was my version of self-harm, and I had a long way to go to heal.

In my pursuit of finding balance, I became a certified yoga instructor in Los Angeles and started teaching classes. I had always been a yoga dilettante, but getting my certification was a challenge for me to take my mind-body health to a new level, and teach others how to do the same.

I found balance through a whole lot of meditation and restructuring my perspective.

There are a lot of tools you can use—both on and off a yoga mat!—to learn how to better walk through the chaos of life and be less consumed by it.

At the end of the day, we're always out of balance. Think about it: even the act of walking means constantly shifting your weight from one foot to

---

[19] For more book recommendations, visit: amysuto.com/six-fig-ure-freelancer

the other, being constantly out of balance, and then adapting to that in order to move forward. If you don't adapt, you fall and get nowhere.

Life is similar. You're constantly having to shift your attention to the next job or the next creative project. You've got a million things to do, and it can be overwhelming.

So, take a minute—stop, and breathe.

Think about the things you're grateful for. Turn to those in your community and in your life and share what's on your mind. Then, do whatever helps you sort through your personal chaos: journal, create action plans, go on a run, or just sit still and let it wash over you and then let it go.

We only have so many days on this planet. Remember, no matter how successful you get or how much money you make, you can never buy your time back. The goal here is to approach each day with lightness and a sense of joy and gratitude. We don't have to be so serious: the goal of this book is to teach you systems and strategies so you can spend more time enjoying your life and work, and not be so burned out you lose interest in what you used to love.

Your time is the most valuable thing you'll ever have in life, so spend it wisely.

Mini-Retirements and Sabbaticals

You don't have to be a professor in order to take a sabbatical, and you don't have to be in your 70s in order to go into a mini "retirement."

Tim Ferriss' book *The Four-Hour Workweek* [20] provides a different take on how to live life and approach work. This was one of the books that changed my perspective on what's possible, and I recommend checking it out if you haven't already. He also touches on the concept of mini-retirements as well.

Essentially, a "mini-retirement" or sabbatical is a length of time (usually greater than six months) that you take off to "retire" and step outside of your day-to-day life. During this time period, you live off of some of your savings and/or passive income streams, and you focus on doing something you love. You might use your mini-retirement to follow an ob-

---

20   For more book recommendations, visit: amysuto.com/six-figure-freelancer

scure indie band on tour or go off-grid and build a cabin with your own two hands. Or, you could just book that trip or spend more time with family and friends right where you are.

These breaks can help you recover from burnout, get recommitted to your work, explore a creative passion, or be a time to learn something new. The perspective you get from taking long periods of time off is unmatched.

Keep these things in mind when planning a mini-retirement or sabbatical:

- **Build up your savings and safety net before you leave.** You don't want to get to zero and lose your financial momentum, so make sure you have enough in the bank before you make the leap. You can also travel to countries that are more affordable if you're wanting to save money.

- **Let your clients know of your plans in advance.** Reach out to your client list and let them know of your plans. Even if you're not actively working with a client, it may be good to give them a heads-up if they want to squeeze in a project with you before you leave.

- **Put up a vacation responder on your email address and post an update on your website or blog.** That way, potential clients can know when you'll be back and when they can resume working with you.

- **Timing matters.** It's probably not wise to plan a year-long backpacking trip when you're just getting started as a freelancer. Instead, try and time your mini-retirement for a place in your life where you don't mind losing some momentum. With that said, if you're in the depths of burnout, the timing for a mini-retirement might be perfect right now.

- **Start with a month.** Does the concept of taking a long time off freak you out? For fellow workaholics, I understand. If you need to, dip your toes in. Start with taking a weekend off, then a week, then a month. See how you feel after that time off, and if you're still burned out or longing for more time to yourself, then pull the trigger if all of the details make sense.

Mini-retirements can make sense in a number of different situations: if you're wanting to have a child and start a family, move to a different country, see the world, or spend time with loved ones—this is a great benefit you can give to yourself as your own boss.

Bouncing Back from Burnout

When bouncing back from burnout, give yourself the time and space to complete the recovery process. Just like we need to take sick days when we're not physically well enough to work, we also have to take "mental health days" when we're not mentally well enough to work.
To deal with burnout, first try to completely disconnect.

If you can, take some time to reflect and journal about why you got burned out. What commitments aren't serving you? Are you putting too much pressure on yourself? How can you ask others for help? Do you need to hire help? Do you need to diversify your schedule or income sources?

Some people have a hard time asking for help. I've heard people describe it as "giving up." But anyone that says that is wrong: to ask for help is *refusing* to give up.

Burnout is a symptom of a greater problem. By identifying the source of discord, we can realign our path and create a better work environment for ourselves moving forward. Self-care isn't just about bubble baths and face masks: it's about identifying your needs as a human and making sure your working environment—both in your creative and freelance work—serves those needs.

✳ Quick Tip: Timing Your Freelance Work to Your Energy Levels

If you're someone who gets periods, chances are your energy takes a nosedive during a certain time every month. While most without ovaries have a 24-hour cycle of energy, people with ovaries tend to have a 28-day cycle and with that comes a variance in energy each week. The secret here? Time your meetings and your work to your 28-day cycle. Maximize meetings during the phase of your cycle when you have the most energy, and spend more time resting, reflecting, and planning when you have less energy. As a freelancer, you have the freedom to make your own schedule, so work with your body—not against it.

Habits to Help You Heal

Burnout is not something you can just "flip a switch" and recover from. It can sometimes take years to unwind the effects of chronic stress and anxiety from your body, and this is especially true if you've been stuck in a traumatic situation and your nervous system has become accustomed to fight-or-flight mode.

Here are my essentials when it comes to burnout recovery:

- **Good daily habits.** A strict daily routine that includes a fifteen-minute walk first thing in the morning (with no sunglasses) to soak in the sun.

- **No coffee.** I gave up coffee and replaced it with matcha oat milk lattes that I make at home. This helped me reduce anxiety and lower my cortisol levels and calm my nervous system (while still getting the benefits of a healthier caffeine source!)

- **Active relaxation and rest.** I spend time on hobbies that promote mindfulness: meditation, journaling, and listening to ASMR/sound healing.

- **Getting a sweat in.** Working out five days a week and getting a minimum of 10,000 steps per day changed my life and my stress response. I try and do cardio twice a week and strength training three times a week every week. You don't need any equipment: there are plenty of free bodyweight workouts you can do at home!

- **Confiding in friends and family.** Freelancing can be lonely, so make sure you're still leaning on your support system of family and friends to get through tough times!

- **Getting to the root cause of stress, overwork, and anxiety.** This book is here to help you deal with overwork so that you can work less and be more effective as a freelancer. However, I've found that sometimes de-stressing requires rewiring a perspective or approach. Even something simple like a daily gratitude practice can help immensely here.

There is no magic pill to solve burnout. It takes daily mindfulness to keep unhealthy habits and stress from overtaking your life.

Amy's Field Notes: Burnout Takes Both a Mental and Physical Toll

Every loud noise made me jump. My body felt jittery even when I didn't drink very much caffeine. My palms sweat for no reason.

These were all symptoms of nervous system dysregulation caused by chronic stress and burnout.

I thought I'd be able to solve my burnout with a few trips to the spa and some extra days off. *Nope.* If it's taken you years to become burned out, it may take you years to unwind the deep effects of chronic stress on your body.

To this day, I'm still clearing out the lasting effects of stress from my body. As I write this, I've been on several weeks of heat and cold therapy—going from hot tub to sauna to cold shower—and staying consistent with my workout routines.

Don't overlook the power of the mind-body connection: when I'm feeling residual stress creep up, I take a break to meditate, do some yoga, and journal. Breathing exercises are your best friend and my go-to. I've never regretted a single minute or dollar I've spent on self-care. None of this *gestures at everything* matters if you're not healthy: both mentally and physically.

    Reframe your priorities and put your well-being at the top of your list. Only then will you be able to reach your true potential in life.

PART 4: BUILDING YOUR IDEAL LIFE AS A FREELANCE WRITER

CHAPTER 28:
FREELANCING WITH A CHRONIC ILLNESS

If you don't have a chronic illness, that's amazing! This chapter is also useful to healthy people to be even healthier. Welcome to my cautionary tale: sit down, make yourself some tea, and gather 'round the fire.

I was diagnosed with the autoimmune disease rheumatoid arthritis at the ripe old age of twenty-seven. It was January 2021, and I was about to embark on my six-month road trip around the US with a bunch of digital nomads in the depths of the pandemic.

My condition happened to hurt me right in the areas I needed to do work every day: my fingers. My early symptoms were swelling in my finger joints and intense pain in my wrists. I swore it must be carpal tunnel, but it wasn't: my genetics and lifestyle at the time betrayed me and I started treatment.

If you suffer from any kind of disease, then you know that those first few months of treatment can be dicey. My hair was falling out with a drug they put me on that's usually prescribed to cancer patients, and I was dealing with intense nausea and dizziness. I had a hard time making it to the end of even an easy hike. My doctor at the time was only being semi-helpful, and I was having to fill in a lot of the gaps of this disease myself. I read books, worked with a nutritionist and personal trainer, threw out all my lifestyle habits, and became a sober vegan. I know, pretty rock-and-roll, right? You don't know how hard this hardcore can be until you do an elimination diet. Eating nothing but raw carrots and spinach all day is not for the faint of heart.

Throughout all of this, I was also maintaining my freelance career. I couldn't fully take time off because I was realizing that rheumatoid arthritis is an *expensive* autoimmune disease.

I don't have to tell you that the American healthcare system is broken: this is common knowledge, and one of the reasons I'm closer to becoming an expat in Europe than ever before. (Europe has my heart for the obvious fact that I can eat bread and cheese there!)

As I was sorting out my health and making changes, I was also learning how to best re-imagine my work/life/health balance. Here's what I have to share if you're wanting to get into freelancing to have a better setup as someone with a chronic illness or disability.

Freelancing vs. Full-Time Jobs for Chronic Illness Warriors

I can say with confidence that my road to recovery was paved with the privilege of not having a full-time job. Being able to work from the couch and take naps when I was tired was clutch during the early days of my illness: I was also dealing with an undiagnosed iron deficiency for months (while at the same time I had just given up coffee so was *very* tired!) and could barely stay awake and was exhausted just walking up the stairs. (*Stairs vs. Amy* was the major showdown in 2021.) Being a freelancer also allowed me to meet virtually with my nutritionist and doctor during the week, and my team of professionals helped me diagnose and treat the root cause of the things that were hurting me.

If I had a traditional full-time job, I wouldn't have had the ability to ramp down my workload or schedule and rest when I needed it. I wouldn't have been able to dip out of a normal 9-to-5 for all those virtual appointments or to drive into town to get a blood test or a refill of my prescription.

A key factor in managing illness is rest. The more sleep you get, the less severe your symptoms are, and the more likely it is that you can put your disease into remission. I was able to get a ton of rest and gentle exercise (such as going on walks or doing yoga!) when my body needed those things during the day. My flexible schedule allowed me to work intuitively when I had the most energy, and rest when I needed it.

Changing my diet was another core part of getting my inflammatory markers down. I'm lucky that my partner Kyle was there to help cook so much great, healthy food for me during those early days, and he helped take care of me when I was having flare-ups or weird symptoms. Having the time and flexibility to eat intuitively and balance my blood sugar with different foods and supplements was also key: something I couldn't have done as easily on an employer-led schedule.

The emotional ups and downs of those early days of my disease were intense. I worried I'd never be able to get my symptoms under control. I felt an incredible lack of knowledge in the face of everything that could have caused my disease to flare. I regretted letting my burnout and workaholism keep me from a healthier lifestyle in the past. I was also so grateful to finally have the time to focus on my health and enforce better decisions moving forward.

Another thing to remember is how freelance gives you the freedom to build a schedule that works for you in a way that full-time office jobs would not. Anyone with a chronic illness knows that the barrage of doctor appointments, blood tests, and afternoon naps required to operate at your best can sometimes be incompatible with a highly competitive in-person job. But as a freelancer, I can be a craftsman and have full control over when and how I work so I can schedule my deep work time when I'm rested and the most productive during my day.

However, I still had to make my freelance workload more manageable and less stressful, and in doing so, I accidentally *doubled* my income and the value I provided to clients while also working less.

So, how on earth do you make your freelance work more balanced and profitable with *less* time and energy–not more?

How to Make Your Freelance Writing Workflow Fit Your Life

Earlier in 2022, I got some not-so-great news from my doctor. My blood test was showing some abnormalities that required further testing, and I was going to have to try out some different medications to see what could help with some of the symptoms I was dealing with.

I took a look at my schedule for the following week. With this news in mind, I started paring back my schedule. Usually, I'm in a reach-for-the-stars mentality: updating my portfolio, writing love letters to companies I want to write for, and jamming on drafts for clients. But when I'm processing bad news or having to start on a new medication, I have to be thoughtful about my bandwidth.

So, when things are hard, consider the following:

- **If you don't relegate all of your meetings to two days per week, consider moving to that schedule.** That way, you can spend the other three workdays doing deep work with rest breaks in-between. Or, you can take a full rest day if your body needs it.

- **If you've got a full roster of clients, consider pausing any client outreach/new client calls.** If you really need a break, put a freeze on any new clients. This might feel counterintuitive, but it's important if you need rest. You need to think more long-term with a chronic condition.

- **Audit your existing projects and clients.** Are there any projects or clients that are deeply stressing you out? Can you weed out any projects that are causing you unnecessary stress and lean into the projects you love?

Reducing work stress is something you have to actively manage as a freelancer with a chronic illness. You can't meditate away an insane schedule or a toxic client: you have to consistently prune your garden and keep maintaining good growth. That's how you'll see the fruits of your labor: through gentle, continuous work and maintenance.

In the next chapter, we'll touch on how to build a year-long calendar of opportunities to help you stay on track as a freelancer!

Amy's Field Notes: I Do Hard Things

There's a pretty good chance that bad things will happen to you or those you love during your life. You might be evacuating from hurricane territory the night of a freelance deadline, or dealing with bad health news right before hopping on a client call.

Sometimes, you have the flexibility to reschedule a call or push a deadline. Sometimes you may not.

On a call with my parents the other day, my dad shared a mantra he liked from the book *Untamed* by Glennon Doyle that he read. It is: *we can do hard things*.

I loved that mantra, and I think it's something you should consider putting up somewhere. *I can do hard things*.

Doing hard things isn't about suffering a miserable existence: it's about making the hard decision now that will create a better life for you in the future. It's about putting in the effort and energy to create a life that works for you, and showing up *every single day* with measured, consistent effort. There are no cheat codes, no hacks. Only strategy and consistency.

Meeting deadlines and turning in great work won't always be easy, which is why you'll have to learn how to reach deep within yourself to do what's needed, especially if you're having a bad day or a tough week... or month.

I don't always feel like hopping on a call with a client, but no matter what's going on in my life, I always show up with a smile. Why? Because I can do hard things, and so can you.

PART 4: BUILDING YOUR IDEAL LIFE AS A FREELANCE WRITER

CHAPTER 29:
THE YEAR-LONG FREELANCE ROADMAP AND OPPORTUNITY CALENDAR

For the first year or two of being a freelancer, you'll likely feel like you're hustling around the clock, and it'll be a big win to carve out work-free weekends and start hitting (and surpassing!) your income goals.

As you settle into your routine of being a full-time freelancer, you'll likely start to notice annual patterns, and be able to plan out your year of opportunity—and rest!—so you can take targeted sabbaticals, vacation when clients are fewer and know when to be available to ramp up and capitalize on a lot of incoming work.

Here's how:

The Annual Calendar of Opportunity

As a freelance writer, I've found that all of my **startup and corporate writing projects** fall into the same patterns:

- I get the biggest increase of **new clients during November-February** as people are wrapping up one year and beginning the next. When budgets are fresh in January (or expiring in December!), corporate/startup clients also seem to spend the most during this period of new year optimism (or are in the end-of-the-year rush!) I have not had a slow holiday season ever in all my years of freelancing. Everyone seems to be extra caffeinated and ready to hire help as they try to reach their goals for the end of one year, or trying to get ahead for the next.

- My **slowest months** are during **May-July**, which is graduation and vacation season. Most companies are run by people with children. Hey, I don't make the rules, it was just the tea leaves I was given. Then, things pick up fast again in late July/early August as kids go back to school and the last two fiscal quarters of the year loom large.

- However, in my **memoir ghostwriting work**, the opposite trend is true: my memoir clients most often hire me in summer when their day jobs are slower and they can devote more time to working on their book with me. I've gotten almost all of my memoir clients during summertime. So, it seems that people prioritize personal needs in the summer, whereas business-related writing work slows down. Diversify your services or plan your budgets based on that information.

- Another interesting trend I've noticed is that there is always an increase in clients **during the beginning/end of months**. This happens as people are realizing the current month is ending/the next month is beginning and they're driven to either make up for lost time or get ahead of the curve, compared to the low-energy middle of the month where new clients dip slightly. People care about beginnings and ends—who knew?

As you're building your freelance career, start to take notice of patterns with clients and client inquiries in your niche. See how they're affected by the economy at large, different seasons, industry trends, and more.

Knowing this will help you organize your efforts and energy to best capture momentum so that you're always booked and as busy as you want to be as a freelancer.

How to Make Your Freelancer's Year Work for You

When you know these patterns, you'll notice your year begins to unlock.

Start to plan your vacations in the middle of the month during slow seasons so you'll feel less guilty turning down incoming leads when you're on holiday. Know when to rest and when to ramp up, and use your annual tracking calendar to monitor the health of your freelance business.

Knowing what's expected during a time of year or month will help you audit a lower-than-expected month. Is May slow because you have fewer clients than usual, or just because all your clients are attending their kids' graduations and planning family vacations?

Part of increasing your revenue as a freelancer is understanding your client base, their needs, and their timing. This will help you make the most of your year and even double your income when you're in step with your calendar of opportunity.

Amy's Field Notes: Digital Nomad Travel Planning

On my website AmySuto.com, you'll find a deep archive of my favorite places to travel as a digital nomad, and tips and tricks for where to stay and what to do in each city!

If you're a freelance writer who loves to travel, use the beginning of the year to plan out your estimated travel budget, where you want to stay, and how much each trip will cost. This will give you something to look forward to, even if you're just planning weekend trips.

As a digital nomad, I try to plan my "fun" travel during the summer when things are slower. That way, I can enjoy being more social and doing things out in the world. At the beginning and end of the year I try to stay in less stimulating places so that I can get deep work done and prioritize focusing on projects I'm working on.

You might not know what's the best flow of your year right away, but that's okay. Over time, you'll start to understand what works best for you and your schedule!

PART 4: BUILDING YOUR IDEAL LIFE AS A FREELANCE WRITER

CHAPTER 30:
BUILDING PASSIVE INCOME

Passive income is any income that requires active initial creation, and then makes money "passively" while you sleep.

This could be through creating a digital download you sell on your blog, or writing a book or a song that pays you through royalties. Or, it could be as ordinary as investing in a stock that pays you dividends, or a rental property that generates monthly revenue.

To be totally candid, passive income is a bit of a myth in the sense that it's not just money you make while you sleep and no effort is required. A digital product or course has to be created, marketed, and updated over time, so some of these "passive" income sources do require strategy and a generous amount of work. Even affiliate marketing links aren't completely effortless: you need an established audience to sell to. If you're buying dividend stocks, you still have to earn the money to buy them in the first place.

However, these sources of income are much more passive than standard freelancing, and if you build them right, you'll be able to scale other sources of cash money so you can enjoy life and take more time off. So, passive income is *not* a magic bullet, but it is a worthy investment of time and money.

Why Freelancers Need Passive Income Sources

As a freelancer, your first priority should be saving for your emergency funds and investing in things like retirement and health insurance benefits. After that, you can start investing time and money into your passive income source of choice.

Building passive income is important for freelancers because it helps to de-risk your work as a freelancer. If you have a slow period, you won't have to dig as deeply into savings if you lose clients or get sick.

Passive income also allows you to travel the world, spend more time with friends and family, and unlock more space in your week for hobbies and creative projects.

However, it takes time to build passive income, so it's best done on the side of your freelancing.

How to Build Passive Income as a Freelancer

As a freelancer, these are the sources of my **active** income:

- Freelance writing
- Freelancer coaching
- Content creation for brands on my blog and social media

As you can tell, all of the above require my active time, energy, and attention. I'm paid to do a job, create content, and make stuff.

Here are some of my sources of **passive** income:

- Digital downloads
- Online courses
- E-Books
- Affiliate links
- Dividends from my stock portfolio

Most of my passive income comes from **knowledge products**. This book is a great example: I'm sharing my knowledge, and readers like you purchase this book because you want to know what I know. After I write and publish the book, my active work is done, and I make money from every sale afterwards.

If you don't have knowledge to share, you could share affiliate links, where you get a percentage of a sale. You can also go a more traditional route, and purchase a dividend stock in the stock market that pays you a certain amount of dividends every so often depending on how many shares you own.

Passive income is infinitely scalable because it's not dependent on your time. This means you could easily be making $500, $1,000, $10,000 or even $100,000 per month with the right passive income plays.

But, as I said, it's no magic bullet: you have to build this over time.

Making Passive Income Building a Part of Your Routine

One of the best ways to build passive income as a freelancer is to simply incorporate it into your routine.

Here are some ideas:

- Invest a small amount into the stock market each month.
- Each week, write a chapter of a book you can publish that shares your unique knowledge.
- Each month, seek out products you use and enjoy and find affiliate links to share with your audience.
- Commit to building an email list and/or social media following so that you have a community to cultivate and market your passive income products to.

Remember, if it sounds too good to be true, it probably is. The only verified get-rich-quick scheme is the lottery, but you don't want to play those odds. Commit to building towards long-term financial security each and every day instead.

Amy's Field Notes: Making Money While I Sleep

I make money while I'm in the jacuzzi. I make money while I'm helping my family make Thanksgiving dinner. I even make money while I sleep.

I first discovered the power of passive income in Rome, Italy. I was feeling rundown by the amount of work I needed to do in my freelancing life and was thinking about everything I'd learned.

So, one afternoon when I had some time in-between assignments, I fired up my laptop camera and started recording short videos and screen-shares that captured my process for finding work on freelancing platforms. I put together all the videos as a course and put them up online. It took me an afternoon or two to put the whole thing together. I didn't have a script or a plan, just a camera and some ideas.

I didn't think anything would come of this little $34.99 course. But now, thousands of students have taken my course and it's a bestseller on Udemy. Some of my students land freelance work forty-eight hours after completing the course!

I don't make an astronomical amount of money from this course. It's meant to be inexpensive and accessible, but because of the volume of people who take my course, I get a nice income stream each month that I don't have to do anything for.

I forget about the course most days–but am always pleasantly surprised by a notification popping up on my phone saying that someone has just purchased the course. Some days, ten or twenty people will purchase it, and I do a little happy dance.

Passive income is work done once that pays out forever. You have valuable, specific knowledge to share: why not get it out there?

PART 4: BUILDING YOUR IDEAL LIFE AS A FREELANCE WRITER

CHAPTER 31:
WHAT TO DO WHEN WORK SLOWS DOWN

I've been at this for months, and I'm going to have to start doing grocery delivery or dog walking if I don't start landing more clients.

I'm doing everything I can, why am I not landing more clients?

Everyone I'm talking to is trying to lowball me. Nobody wants to pay my rates.

My income is down for the third month in a row and rent is coming up and I can barely pay it. What do I do?

As freelancers, these are scary, anxiety-attack-inducing thoughts that come with the feast-or-famine cycle that freelancing can be.

Freelancing can feel more volatile in the beginning. But if you build a foundation to support yourself when the occasional dips occur in the freelance job market, you won't sweat a slower month and might even *enjoy* the downtime. Here's how to build a freelancing career that allows you to weather the ups and downs while still keeping your bills paid and a roof over your head.

Foundations to Build When Work is Flowing

The feeling of an "up" month can be intoxicating, especially as you crush your goals and become fully booked. The *cha-ching* of incoming work and invoices paid is such a rush. It's a chance to celebrate—and to start saving for the future.

When you're hitting your income targets, consider doing the following:

- **Pay off any credit cards or high-interest debt.** Most personal finance books will direct you to pay off any high-interest debt first. This is generally a good rule of thumb depending on what your financial situation is as high-interest debt can hurt you in the long run.

- **Contribute to emergency funds.** Your personal and business bank accounts should have six months' savings to cover your bare essential expenses. Before you start investing back into your business, invest in your most important asset: safety and stability. Everyone's financial strategy is different—so talk to a CPA if you need guidance—but in my mind, I've always prioritized having a healthy emergency fund before I do anything else.

- **Hire support staff.** By hiring a virtual assistant or other support staff, you can start freeing up more of your time to go after more freelance work or spend time developing sources of passive income.

- **Revamp your website and marketing materials.** When I hired a web designer to redo my website, the results were awesome. I was able to book more leads directly through my website and sell more digital downloads, so the investment paid for itself in a matter of months. I also had a professional designer design my freelance portfolio. First impressions matter, so when you get the chance to work with experts—or invest your time into learning how to do design!—it can lead to more conversions of potential clients.

- **Write more on your blog.** Invest your time into writing more articles for your blog so you can generate more passive leads from your website. Bonus points if you also start getting on a press newsletter[21] to help journalists who need sources, and get backlinks to your blog in the process (which boosts your search engine rankings!)

---

21 For my current recommendations on newsletters to pitch to journalists, visit: amysuto.com/six-figure-freelancer

- **Revisit your personal policies.** You could potentially save more by bundling vision, dental, life insurance, and health insurance and covering them through your business, especially if you have at least one employee. Contact a health insurance broker in your state and see what your options are. This could pay off if you're able to save on insurance costs by shopping around in private marketplaces and paying for it through your business. Some policies require you to have employees for this to be possible, so be aware of what your options are and don't hesitate to do your research.

- **Invest in automation tools.** Invest your time and money into figuring out how to continue to automate your workflow, and revisit the automation chapter of this book for more tips on how to do this!

- **Join a co-working space.** An investment into a co-working space membership can help you meet fellow freelancers and potential clients under one roof. It can also create a better work/life balance, especially if you and your partner or roommate both work from home.

- **Beef up your personal investment portfolio.** Consider investing in stocks, real estate, or other passive income-producing assets.

At the end of the day, it's up to you to decide what to do with your profits. Talk to your CPA to create a plan-of-action for your finances that works best for you and your lifestyle!

What to Do in a Down Month

Let's start with the first signs that your work as a freelancer is slowing down: your income is down this month.

First, assess how far in the red you are. Is your work just dipping from a recent high? Is it summer and your work is just in a seasonal slowdown as people take time to rest and vacation with family? Or is it during a usually busy time of the year and you're seeing a sharp decrease?

Next, figure out what's going on with the markets. People and businesses are often swayed by the stock market, so if things aren't looking good then you can probably point to the stock market as a good reason why they're not hiring a bunch of freelance help right now. After all, the stock market is just a graph of rich people's feelings.

If the markets are good and you're having a down month during what is usually a busy season for you, it's time to do some more digging and take appropriate action.

Scenario #1: Losing a Big Client

Losing a big client or recurring work can hurt, especially if it's an unexpected loss. If this happens, first get your mindset right: this client left space in your schedule for you to find a better client who you'll love working with even more.

This is also a good chance to remember to keep your income diverse as a freelancer: one client shouldn't be a majority of your income. If they are, it's just a reminder that you need more projects, and if that feels overwhelming, it may be time for you to raise your per-project price.

Anytime I've lost big clients, I've just used the extra time to work on passive income projects, cold email new clients I want to work with, and step up outreach on freelance platforms. This also might be a good opportunity to diversify your marketing by attending a conference or an in-person or online networking event where your ideal clients hang out, and post more on social media or your blog.

Scenario #2: Losing Most Clients from a Market Correction

When COVID hit in 2020, I had just left my last writers' room and was full-time freelance. Almost all of my clients either paused or canceled contracts because of COVID, and at first, it was super scary to see everything dry up so quickly. During those first two months of the pandemic, I took time to post more on my blog, hone my craft, read more books, and work on personal projects.

As everyone adapted to the new pandemic reality, work came back in full-force and in May of 2020, I was overbooked and raising my rates with every new client. Everyone was ready to write their memoir or start that business, and the shutdown ended up being a huge boon for business.

The same thing happened during the writing of this book in 2022. I saw record-high months for my work as a web3 copywriter in January-March of this year. But when crypto started to crash along with the rest of the markets, I saw some clients canceling their plans and backing down from contracts they were just about to sign with me. It seemed like my work was headed into a slowdown as my niche in particular saw the effects of the crash. Is crypto rich people's feelings, too?

In reality, I'm still fully committed with clients and haven't seen too much of a slowdown since the crash. My summers are generally a bit slower with the season, but I'm still booking $12,000 weeks even with the insane market conditions and uncertainty, and layoffs that are happening all over tech.

The lesson here is that, sometimes, freelance jobs are safer than "stable" full-time jobs. When it's time to do budget cuts, companies usually go for full-time employees first. Freelance talent is already seen as a flexible expense, and part of a (very large!) marketing budget. And when the marketing team needs help, hiring freelancers usually feels like a cost-saving measure.

If the economy is crashing, don't panic. Stay the course and keep moving forward: the momentum might just need a beat to pick back up, and this is why building your emergency fund is so important.

What to Do in a Down Quarter

Let's say your down month turns into a down quarter. Your savings start to dwindle and your work is still keeping you in the red.

Here are some things to consider:

- **Is your productivity down? If so, why?** You're not a robot, so you can't be expected to operate at crazy levels of productivity year-round, but if you're seeing a massive drop in your ability to handle outreach and stay steady on your blog writing, then there might be an underlying reason. This could be burnout, sickness, mental health issues, or general blocks in your emotional world keeping you from doing the work you need to get done and staying on track with client outreach. Find the root cause of this: take a vacation, see a therapist, focus on your health and fitness, check in with your doctor, or journal on why you've been feeling out of it or down lately.

- **Audit your excitement about your niche.** Are you sick of your niche? If so, it may be time to dabble in a new niche. When I got burned out from memoir ghostwriting which was my sole focus for a year, I switched my focus to copywriting with some ghostwriting on the side, and my energy came roaring back.

- **Examine your services.** You might not even need to switch niches: you could even just add or remove services to your list. This could be as simple as getting rid of a type of service that is draining you (such as social media writing) and focusing on something you're more passionate about (like long-form article writing or book ghostwriting.)

- **Redo your schedule.** Maybe poor time management is keeping you overworked and burned out. Or, you might be lacking in the activities that bring you to life, which is making you feel tired and overworked. Rework your schedule, and try some of the tips I've offered in early chapters when it comes to preventing burnout or try out a maker/manager day schedule.

- **Raise/lower your prices or offer discounted package pricing.** I'm never an advocate of lowering your pricing, even during low months. However, if you're struggling with low demand of your services and keep getting feedback that your price is too high, you can consider lowering your prices or offering a discount to new clients to entice them to try working with you. Before you do that, though, try offering a fixed-rate package rate to potential new clients that offers an inherent discount with bundled services. This will allow you to maintain the integrity of your hourly rate while trying out a discounted rate. Everybody loves a discount. Alternatively, if you're burned out and can't keep up with client demand, it's time to raise your rates. Even if you lose clients, you'll be making the same or more money which will free up time and reduce burnout.

- **Expand marketing of your services.** Get on social media and share more about what you do. Livestream on social media and talk about topics related to your expertise and include clear call-to-actions so people know how they can hire you. Keep on making informative content that will drive clients to want to work with you, and get creative with your reach-outs and potential client research.

A down quarter can feel like you're losing, but it might just be an indicator that your current strategies, pricing, or services aren't working. Use it as an opportunity to either double down and stay the course, or to pivot if you feel like your services aren't retaining clients or leading to more work.

If the down quarter is related to the economy, some freelancers opt to take on part-time jobs. Personally, I find this is an easy way to get burned out, and instead would recommend expanding your passive income projects so you can have consistent, recurring revenue that comes in while you sleep.

What to Do in a Down Year

If it's been a full year of freelancing with low-income months, you might feel like it's time to quit freelancing altogether.

If you've been employing all the bullet points I've outlined above for every scenario and keeping your energy and productivity up, then I would recommend staying the course as a freelancer.

Instead, think about:

- **Are robots taking your work?** Artificial intelligence-based software might be encroaching on lower-paid copywriting jobs like keyword-stuffed, content mill-created blog posts. If this is the case, try and specialize in a more complex, high-level niche. This is part of the reason I specialize in storytelling and creative copywriting in web3 and memoir ghostwriting. Robots can't tell good stories (yet!) in a way that also explains the features of a game or tells someone's life story, so my work is still safe from the robots… for now.

- **Are you in a race to the bottom with your pricing?** If you're trying to compete as a freelancer in the "who can charge less" game, you're probably going to lose out to remote talent willing to work for *even less* than you. Never doubt humanity's ability to have lower standards. If this is the case, try and specialize in a niche that prizes your critical thinking and cultural knowledge.

- **Is your niche becoming obsolete?** If you're a freelance writer who specialized in writing about fax machine products, you might be struggling for work in this day and age. If your focus and portfolio are geared towards an industry or subject that is becoming irrelevant, it might be time to start to retool your focus and stop using a landline.

- **Am I dealing with a chronic illness or mental illness that is making freelance a challenge for me?** As someone who developed rheumatoid arthritis that created swelling and pain in my finger and wrist joints, this posed a real problem for me. I solved this by expanding my freelance business to include support staff assistants and targeted outsourcing of aspects of my process. I'm not an expert on understanding disability insurance/government benefits, but that may be something to explore as well depending on where you live and what insurance you have for yourself and your business.

- **Are my expenses outpacing my earnings?** Take a look at your personal and business expenses. Is the reason why you're not profitable because you're spending too much? Ideally, freelancing should be able to cover your expenses no matter where you're at, but if you're struggling with "lifestyle creep" and ballin' with bottle service too frequently, you may want to consider making a change when it comes to some of your highest expenses.

Journal on some of the questions above and do some more digging to figure out the causes of what's been going on. It may be time to cut off that Nigerian Prince. They rarely make due on their promises.

Freelancing can be feast-or-famine, but if you're constantly in famine, there's something else going wrong.

"Failing" at Freelancing and When to Quit

I believe that freelancing is for everyone, but I know there are people who disagree with me. Some people say that they like the routine of a 9-5 job, guaranteed weekends and vacations, and stable benefits.

So, if you're finding yourself missing your routine or office job, then maybe freelancing isn't working for you in a way that fits in with your ideal lifestyle. There's no shame in going back to a full-time job, or getting a part-time job and returning freelancing to a "side hustle" status in your life. Your freelance portfolio can also help you potentially land a better, higher-paying job.

If you're looking for a better setup as a freelancer, you also might want to consider freelancing or doing full-time work for a marketing agency. This can help with stability even if it may pay less than your work as a freelancer.

Another option is that you could take a break from freelancing and pursue full-time work until you've figured out what's been going wrong with your freelancing business. You could return after you've developed a new skillset or changed niches.

Before you decide to quit, you could also consider consulting with a more experienced freelancer or a freelance coach. I offer coaching for freelancers who need outside help, and you can reach out to me at amy@amysuto.com if you're needing one-on-one guidance and additional resources.

At the end of the day, freelancing has to be profitable for it to make sense in your life. If you're constantly in the red, then it may be time to pursue a different path.

I've dealt with my fair share of failures—this work is not easy. But if wins are seldom and heartbreak is common, it might be time to chart a new course.

It takes bravery to make a change that's the best for you and your health and happiness. Have the courage to make the hard choice, whether that's to pivot within your freelancing career or to start a new journey altogether.

If you're able to stick with it and pave a path to success—amazing! In the next (and last!) chapter of the book, we'll talk about how to capitalize on and leverage momentum to set you up for life.

One last ride?

One last ride.

Amy's Field Notes: Jobs That Fall from the Sky

When work seems to be slowing down for me, the old scarcity mindset tries to rear its ugly head.

Then, without fail, *every single time*, a huge job lands from the sky.

It's funny at this point: the moment doubt starts to creep up...

...it's immediately replaced by a new project or client.

Momentum is an interesting thing. It takes care of you in mysterious ways. I see this with other freelancers also: if you put in the work and make yourself findable, the right clients will stumble upon your writing and want to hire you.

Keep going: the sun always rises, after all.

PART 4: BUILDING YOUR IDEAL LIFE AS A FREELANCE WRITER

CHAPTER 32:
LEVERAGING SUCCESS AS A FREELANCER

You've done it: you've optimized your marketing, automated your workflow, honed your craft by learning every day, and made it to the end of this book. You've prevented or recovered from burnout, and clients are banging down your door even after you raise your rates time and time again. You're a successful freelancer and each year you're seeing your annual income grow, which gives you more time and energy to reinvent yourself and your business while securing your future.

First, take a moment to cherish your success. Your hard work is bearing fruit, and that's an awesome position to be in.

Where to Next?

Once you've built a successful freelancing career, there are a lot of options as far as your next steps are concerned. Here are some of them:

- **Build an agency.** As we've covered earlier in this book, you can increase your services and grow your client base by adding more freelancers or employees to support you as you scale into an agency.

- **Create a speaking/author career.** Do you have a story or a cause you're passionate about? You can write books and get paid to speak about your special sauce. This can be in the form of workshops, paid speaking gigs, and more. You can reach out to different places to speak at events and conferences, and you can also host workshops in your city to help share your unique knowledge.

- **Create a coaching/educator career.** If you're an expert at something, you can also sell your knowledge in the form of a course, a book like this one, or you can start a social media channel and monetize through ad revenue. This is what I do, and I help writers get into freelancing by creating online content and writing books like this! It's so fulfilling to be able to help others do this work, so if you're naturally drawn to mentoring and creating educational materials, this could be a great path.

- **Build an artist's life.** Instead of scaling your freelancing, you can invest/save your income, keep your expenses low, and pursue an artist's life. Go to museums, write that novel, put on that play, and create your own projects. These projects may one day pay the bills, or not. That's the beauty of freelance work: you can maintain more artistic integrity if you don't desperately need your art to sell because you've got your freelance income to pay your bills.

- **Build a founder's life.** You can also use your work to build up connections and network with other freelancers and build a startup together. Use your freelancing to cover bills and bootstrap your business, or raise VC funding and eventually quit freelancing altogether, maybe creating a consulting business on the side as an additional income source. Freelancing pairs pretty well with a founder's life, although you have to be wary of burnout if you're also investing in your own business.

- **Invest and "retire" early.** Is leisure and travel time your ultimate goal? You can achieve this in any of the above options, but it can be your main focus if you want it to be. Figure out how to travel to conferences for your work so you can write off more tax deductions for travel, and become a travel points hacker to figure out how to travel for cheap. Invest in property and create pockets of retirement for yourself, or get on a path to retire early.

PART 4: BUILDING YOUR IDEAL LIFE AS A FREELANCE WRITER

Everything you do should be in service of doing more of what you love, and less of what you don't! So, try and figure out what that ideal day-to-day looks like for you, even if that means eventually leaving freelancing behind you forever.

Moving on From Freelancing

You won't be freelancing forever—and that's a good thing. Freelancing is a service business: it requires customer service, a deep knowledge of your craft, and active attention and cultivation to keep it going.

Deciding when to sunset your freelancing career depends on a number of factors. Your niche may grow boring, or you may get tired of writing in a particular form. Or, you might raise your prices so high you only take on a few clients a year, and that's ideal so you can focus on other projects or pursuits in your life.

When you're done freelancing, you will probably still get leads in from clients who have heard about you who want to work with you. Consider "paying it forward" and meet new freelancers you can refer these leads to. Help new writers get their foothold in their freelancing careers, even if you never received the same support.

You've Made It

I wrote this book because freelancing has changed my life, and I know it has the potential to change yours if it hasn't already.

For these final words, I just want to offer a piece of encouragement. *Don't give up, just regroup.*

This path is a long one. Success is determined by what you do every day. Becoming a six-figure freelance writer is no different.

I'm excited for you and the life you're about to build for yourself.

Enjoy.

Amy's Field Notes: There Must Be Something Better

When I was just getting started as a freelance writer, I was trapped in a miserable minimum-wage job. I was working for a manipulative boss in a toxic work environment, and I was desperate to find my next career move. I was losing an unhealthy amount of weight, working insane hours, and anxiety would wash over me every Sunday night as I dreaded the workweek with a pit in my stomach. I would talk to co-workers on our lunch break who were as beaten down as I was, trying to understand why life was so difficult for us.

There must be something better.

The first few times I said this, I didn't totally believe it. A part of me wondered if the only way I could survive was with a soul-sucking job. Maybe the reality of being an adult is that work just sucks. Your boss is horrible. Your co-workers are partying on weekends and drinking every night to dull the barbs and mind games dished out by management every day. Isn't that just how life is, and you grin and bear it?

But I was still in my early twenties, and the glimmer of hope remained, even as I was passed up for opportunities and got what I thought could have been "dream jobs" ripped away from me.

There must be something better.

I read books where authors said they had manifested better jobs, better lives. And then I read books saying how the system is rigged if you're not already wealthy, so why bother?

It was hard to know who to trust. Were these entrepreneur authors just telling me what I wanted to hear when they said I could build wealth and control my own destiny? Were they just trying to sell books? But I wanted to believe.

There must be something better.

I built a few small businesses and failed, but learned sales and marketing from those failures.

There must be something better.

I quit Hollywood and threw myself into freelancing, but was working crazy hours and still had some nightmare clients.

There must be something better.

I raised my rates, got better at picking clients, and developed systems.

There must be something better.

I started traveling, learned about how to optimize my freelance business, and started working less.

There must be something better.

There is. And I found it.

Today, I'm living a dream. I met my soulmate Kyle and we spend most of our time traveling and seeing the world. I now only work fifteen to twenty hours per week on my freelance business, but am on track to break seven-figure freelancer status in the near future. A younger version of myself would look at my life, tears in her eyes, and with a look of awe would say: thank you for never giving up. You found our "something better."

Something better is right around the corner. Turning that corner may not be easy or instant, but once you do, everything changes.

Go find your *something better*.

PART 4: BUILDING YOUR IDEAL LIFE AS A FREELANCE WRITER

CHAPTER 33:
THE NEVER-ENDING CHAPTER

Okay, okay–I didn't want to say goodbye just yet. Welcome to the real final chapter of the book: the *never-ending chapter*.

This chapter was my partner Kyle's idea, and he graciously let me use it.

You won't find this chapter in this book. Instead, I'll add a new never-ending chapter each year to my digital appendix: amysuto.com/six-figure-freelancer

On that secret page of my website, you'll find all of the resources mentioned in this book as well as a yearly update to the never-ending chapter.

I've done this because freelancing evolves over time: new platforms and tools evolve, and current events impact the way freelancers do their work.

The contents of this book are evergreen: strategies that stand the test of time. But the never-ending chapter will be your resources for how to become a six-figure freelancer in the here and now.

Good luck on your journey, fellow travelers.

Acknowledgments

Thank you to my partner-in-crime, Kyle Cords. Your editorial eye keeps me striving to hit higher standards (and punchier jokes!) in my work. Thanks to Jack Bentele for taking the time to give your perspective as a fellow writer in this world. Thanks to Ashley Munson for bringing your artistic talent to the cover and interior of this book, and to Dana Alsamsam for proofreading and formatting this book to perfection. Lastly, thanks to my parents who have always supported my dreams and encouraged my love of writing.

About the Author

Amy Suto began her career as a Hollywood TV writer before hitting the road and becoming a digital nomad and six-figure freelance writer. She specializes in serving clients as a memoir ghostwriter and writes books for professional athletes, Silicon Valley CEOs, and other inspiring individuals. Amy taps into her seven years of professional storytelling experience to help her clients become bestselling authors and TED speakers. When she's not writing, Amy travels the world and works remotely from cafes in Prague—or is misplacing her AirPods in Lisbon. You can learn more about Amy at: Amy-Suto.com.

Printed in Great Britain
by Amazon